GREAT TALES FROM BRITISH HISTORY

ON THE EVE OF THE TITANIC DISASTER

W. B. BARTLETT

AMBERLEY

First published 2014

Amberley Publishing
The Hill, Stroud
Gloucestershire, GL5 4EP

www.amberley-books.com

British Library Cataloguing in Publication Data.
A catalogue record for this book is available from the British Library.

ISBN 978 1 4456 4368 7 (paperback)
ISBN 978 1 4456 4401 1 (ebook)

Typeset in 9.75pt on 12pt Minion Pro.
Typesetting and Origination by Amberley Publishing.

Printed in the UK.

Collision

23.40, 14 April 1912, North Atlantic
49 Degrees 57 Minutes West, 41 Degrees
44 Minutes North

Titanic steamed through the darkness of the night, her sharp prow cutting through the chill water like a knife through butter. Despite the warnings of ice ahead, the ship was going at nearly 22 knots, as fast as she had ever been and indeed as fast as she would ever go. The decks were quieter now, a somniferous hand had descended over the ship and most people had turned in for the night. Few were abroad on this cold night, with the temperatures plummeting and the air icy.

But a small number of those onboard were still wide awake. High up in the crow's nest, lookouts Frederick Fleet and Reginald Lee peered intently into the inky blackness. The stars were bright but were of little help in picking anything out. Ahead of them, everything bore an ebony hue, with no disruption at all to the monotone darkness apart from the diamond-like stars high above. At sea level, there was nothing. No sign of any ice, no sign of a wave, no sign even of another ship's light. Lee remembered seeing a haze on the horizon. He was insistent that Fleet said to him that 'if we can see through that, we will be lucky'. However Fleet denied ever saying any such thing and Lord Mersey, Chairman of the subsequent British Inquiry, thought this was a too convenient explanation to justify not spotting any ice until it was too late.

Able Seaman Joseph Scarrott was on watch, which as a sailor meant that he was basically on call awaiting whatever instructions might emanate from the bridge. He heard the bells struck for 11.30 p.m., and a few minutes passed without any interruption to the dull monotony of life onboard a great liner at night. No parties or *haute cuisine* for these men, just a series of unexciting chores. It was approaching 11.40 p.m., just another three-quarters of an hour before knocking-off time and the promise of a warm bunk down below, especially appreciated by the lookouts in their lofty eyrie. It would not be a moment too soon. It was a perishing cold night, and steamy vapour trails came out like the breath of a dragon every time they exhaled.

Suddenly, Fleet was shaken to the core. There ahead, looming out of the darkness, some 500 yards ahead, something lay directly in their path. Given the coldness of the air, given the warnings they had received earlier, it could only be one thing – ice. At first it was not that big, just the size of two tables as Fleet later recalled (it would become clear during subsequent investigations that he was not a good judge of distance or scale). However, as they came closer, it grew in stature until it was something very large indeed.

As the berg loomed into view, Fleet frantically rang three bells – the signal for an object dead ahead – and rushed to the telephone that connected the crow's nest to the bridge. The answer came quickly, said Fleet, a simple 'What do you see?' from Sixth Officer Moody. Fleet gasped out: 'Iceberg, right ahead!' (though first-class passenger Major Peuchen, in evidence at the American Inquiry, would say that Fleet had told *him* that he did not get an immediate reply when he rang the phone). Almost simultaneously, Murdoch had spotted the berg from the bridge and was already starting to take evasive action.

The forty seconds that followed were the longest of Fleet's life. Each second seemed to last an hour and yet the leviathan still did not move (some later suggested that the rudder was too small for the size of the ship). She seemed to dart straight as an arrow for the berg. Then at the last moment she slowly started to turn away. She began to swing with agonizing lethargy to port but it was too late, far too late, and she struck just before the foremast. There was just the faintest grinding noise that Fleet could hear but no noticeable jar. To him, it was nothing more than 'a narrow shave'. However, Lee distinctly heard a 'rending of metal' as the berg scraped along the ship's side.

In reality it was anything but a close shave. It was in retrospect a pity that she moved off line at all, though of course it was completely natural that the ship's navigators should try and escape a collision. A head-on crash would have stoved in the bows and undoubtedly led to loss of life but most of the watertight compartments would have been unaffected. She would certainly have listed but would probably have floated. However, the apparent glancing blow had torn holes in her side which compromised the integrity of a number of the watertight compartments. In truth, whatever anyone did now, the ship was doomed. It had taken years to plan and build her. It had taken just seconds to condemn her to oblivion.

When Murdoch had seen the berg, instructions were sent down at once to the engine rooms. Far down below in Boiler Room 6 as in all others a series of lights gave automated instructions to those working in the bowels of the ship as to what was expected of them; white meant full speed ahead, blue slow and red stop. A red light flashed on. Leading stoker Fred Barrett was in charge and immediately shouted to his men to 'shut all dampers'. His men rushed to comply but before they could fully do so there was a crash.

On the bridge, the man with his hand on the helm was Quartermaster Hichens. As the berg loomed inexorably closer, closing in on him as if he were about to run headfirst into a wall, Murdoch frantically shouted to him to try and steer around it. Hichens responded: 'Hard astarboard. The helm is hard over.' Then came the blow.

Slight though it may have been, Captain Smith was already rushing out of his cabin to find out what the problem was. 'What is it?' he asked. 'An iceberg,' responded Murdoch. 'I put her hard astarboard and ran the engines full astern, but it was too close; she hit it.' He explained that he planned to port round the iceberg and then put the helm hard over the other way so that the stern of the ship would swing clear but that she had been too close to avoid the berg. Captain Smith told his First Officer to shut the watertight doors but Murdoch responded that he had already done so. Smith looked at the commutator, which measured if the ship had any list; within a few minutes it told him that she was already listing 5 degrees to starboard.

Questions would later be asked about the *Titanic*'s lookout arrangements. For example, the lack of binoculars in the crow's nest later became a bone of contention. Lookouts Hogg and Evans had asked for them in Southampton but were told there were none though they had had them on the way over from Belfast. Hogg was later interviewed and was surprised that they were not issued to them, thinking that they would have made a difference. Fleet would later be asked if he could have spotted the ice earlier with binoculars.

He would insist that 'we could have seen it a bit sooner'. When asked how much sooner, he responded pointedly: 'Well, enough to get out of the way.'

It was a point of view not shared by Second Officer Lightoller. He actually considered that binoculars were detrimental to the lookouts. However, there is an element of self-defence in this assertion perhaps. It was the Second Officer's job to know where the binoculars were and, with Lightoller taking over the role from Davy Blair at the last moment, this piece of knowledge had been lost. But others also thought 'glasses' were of limited value, such as Seaman Thomas Jones, who had served as a lookout on other ships though not on the *Titanic*. Lookout Archie Jewell on the other hand thought that they were 'very useful'.

There was also the lookout's positioning to take into account. Sir Ernest Shackleton had described how he always posted lookouts in the bows of the ship when looking for ice (a strategy that Captain Rostron, master of the rescue ship *Carpathia*, would employ later that night). Captain Lord had done the same. Yet Captain Smith did not think this was necessary, He had gambled on a normal lookout service spotting the ice before he reached it and he had lost. The price of the forfeit would be enormous.

Across the ship, the collision registered in many different ways to many different people. The majority of those aboard felt little, though it depended to a great extent on where you were; those lower down and on the starboard side where the collision happened felt a much greater force than those elsewhere.

For example, Lawrence Beesley had been lying in his bed reading and had suddenly been conscious that the vibrations of the ship seemed to increase. The mattress was his usual indicator of such things and now it seemed to be a stronger sensation of rocking in it than he had ever felt before. It made him think that the ship was moving more quickly than ever. Outside his room, he had heard the muffled voices of stewards talking in the corridors as he started to get drowsy. And then he felt something, a disturbance to the regular running of the engines and an increase to the vibrations.

Jack Thayer was winding his watch and about to retire when he felt the ship sway. She had veered to port, as if she had been gently pushed. The shock was very slight, so much so that if he had have been holding a glass of water he was confident he would not have spilt a drop.

Little Eva Hart was in her cabin with her family, in a comfortable four-berth with a table her nervous mother used for her sewing. Her mother had been worried about being on the ship from the start and had refused to sleep in a bed at night. She later described how she felt a little 'bump'. It did not register very strongly because the cabin was on the portside, far away from the point of collision. She straight away woke Eva's father up. He went away at once to find out what had happened and came back, reporting the accident to his family. He would later tell them that they were going to launch the boats but they should not worry too much, for he was sure they would all be back onboard for breakfast.

Asleep in his cabin adjacent to the wireless shack, Harold Bride did not realize that there had been a collision at all. He got up as planned just before midnight to relieve Phillips who had been very busy. Phillips told him that he thought the ship had been damaged and would probably have to return to Belfast for repairs (perhaps he was aware of a practical problem; there was no dry dock in the USA big enough to deal with the *Titanic*).

Bride had planned to be up earlier than usual, as it had been a particularly trying day. The problem with the apparatus had taken them seven hours to fix. At last, after trial and error, they found that one of the components had burnt out and replaced it. The timely discovery and fixing of the problem was one of the few strokes of luck that the *Titanic* experienced that night. The thought of the *Titanic* being without her wireless at this crucial moment does not bear thinking about.

There were three rooms in the wireless shack: a sleeping room, a dynamo room and an operating room. Bride, tired, had soon fallen asleep when he went to bed but had later woken, to hear Phillips sending passenger chit-chat to the shore station at Cape Race. When the iceberg was struck, he felt no shock or jolt at all. He was barely aware that anything had happened.

Fifth Officer Harold Lowe was also not woken by the impact and slept on until he heard the sounds of voices outside of his door. He was amazed when he went out on deck and saw people milling around with lifebelts on. He got up and noticed something strange about the ship. When someone later suggested at the Inquiries that she was listing he corrected the statement; she was, he said, 'tipping', not listing, that is angling forward rather than sideways. Lowe was a cautious man and at some stage went into his cabin and picked up his revolver just in case it might be needed.

Quartermaster George Rowe was on watch towards the stern of *Titanic* when the collision came. He saw a massive berg float past, at first thinking it was a close shave with a sailing ship. However, the seriousness of the situation did not dawn on him at all. He went back on watch and while throughout the rest of the ship the drama unfolded, he was oblivious to what was happening. He would later see a lifeboat go past at around half past midnight and telephoned the bridge to report it. Incredulous, they asked him to report to the bridge. Rowe, the last person to find out perhaps that they were in trouble, would later play a part in firing off distress rockets.

Lightoller was about to fall asleep when he was shaken awake by a vibration passing the whole length of the ship. It was not a violent sensation. However, there had been such a distinct lack of vibration during the trip so far that the break to the mundane smoothness was enough to disturb him. He was up in a second. Not bothering to throw on anything over his pyjamas he ran first to the port side of the ship, then the starboard. He could see nothing in the icy darkness and with the frigid air biting into him gratefully made his way back to his warm bunk.

Others tried to see the berg too but few were able to. One exception was Steward Crawford who went out and saw the iceberg, 'a large black object, much higher than B Deck, passing along the starboard side'. In contrast, Pierre Maréchal, son of a vice-admiral of the French navy, Lucien Smith, Paul Chevré, a French sculptor and A. F. Omont, a cotton broker, were playing bridge in the Café Parisien when the ship struck. They went outside, looked over the edge to see if they could spot the cause of the collision, and then returned to their card game having failed to do so. One returned to the café to pick up his cigar, which he had left burning there, saying that he couldn't waste it. None of them thought that the collision was serious. Maréchal was among the survivors, as was Chevré and Omont. They all had winning hands that night, unlike Smith who perished.

Third Officer Pitman was in bed when the collision came; it woke him up. It seemed to him as if the ship was coming to anchor. He dressed and went outside but he saw or heard nothing. So unperturbed was he that he went back to his quarters and lit himself a pipe. Steward Edward Wheelton, perhaps remembering what had happened to the *Olympic* not too long before (just back in February), thought that the ship had dropped a propeller. He thought it would mean a trip back to Belfast for repairs.

Many people were unperturbed by the accident, barely noticing it at all. However, some were more concerned by it. Governess Elizabeth Shute noticed that 'suddenly a queer shivering ran under me, apparently the whole length of the ship'. The strangeness of the sensation disturbed her and she jumped out of bed. However, excessively reassured by the sheer magnitude of the ship she was on, she went back to bed but it was just a very short space of time before a friend from a nearby cabin knocked on her door and told her to get up. She told her that they had struck an iceberg; if she was quick she might still be able to catch sight of it out of the window.

The collision also made a strong impression on Edith Brown. She was asleep but felt a great vibration cause the ship to shiver as if in fear. Colonel Gracie was 'enjoying a good night's rest when I was aroused by a sudden shock and noise forward on the starboard side, which I at once concluded was caused by a collision, with some other ship perhaps'. He jumped from his bed and turned on the light. He glanced at his clock, which he had not yet reset; it said it was midnight (Gracie thought this made it about 11.45 p.m. ship's time). He went out into corridor but could see no one. However, there was 'a great noise of escaping steam'. Most noticeably, the ship had stopped.

At the time of the collision, Charlotte Collyer was getting ready for bed. It felt to Charlotte as if the ship had been picked up by a giant hand and shaken a couple of times before she came to a halt. Charlotte felt a long backward jerk, followed by a shorter one. Despite the sensation, she was not thrown out of her bed and her husband stood steady on his feet. There were no strange sounds, no noises of steel being ripped, but the main thing they noticed was a negative sensation, the lack of motion as the ship stopped.

It was the crew and third-class passengers, furthest down in the ship's bowels, who experienced the greatest shock. When the ship struck, Seaman W. Brice heard a rumbling that lasted 'about ten seconds'. George Beauchamp, a fireman who was on duty at the time, heard a noise that was 'like thunder, the roar of thunder'.

The boiler rooms were the most obviously affected. In Boiler Room 6 there was a tremendous bang and the starboard side of the ship was pierced. Water started to rush in from a hole about 2 feet above floor level (it was later estimated that this was about 24 feet below sea level). Men had to jump under the rapidly closing watertight doors to escape. They planned to return but when Fireman Barrett climbed back towards Boiler Room 6 he could not get back in it for it was already under about 8 feet of water – this in the space of just about ten minutes.

He had no doubts at all about the seriousness of the crash. If the water rose by 14 feet in total, just another 6 feet, it would come up through the plates of the floor above and then slop over into the next watertight compartment. It would inevitably pull the *Titanic* down by the head. He had already looked in the coal bunker on the other side of the watertight compartment, a vast, cavernous space, capable of holding 500 tons of coal. It was empty and he could see that water was coming in – he likened it to the flow of water one might see coming out of a fire hose. At any event, the *Titanic's* hull had been breached even beyond Boiler Room 6 and there was no doubt that she was in serious trouble.

The nature of the damage caused by the collision has been made clearer by the discovery of the wreck. Dives on the ship have located some of the iceberg damage. The *Titanic* was held together by wrought iron rivets rather than welded as a modern ship would be, with the plates of the ship overlapping each other. When the ship collided with the berg, the effect of the collision was to 'pop' the rivets, causing the plates of steel that they had held together to part. Through the gap created as a result, water started to stream in.

The rivets were made of wrought iron, a mix of iron and slag. If there was too high a proportion of slag, that would compromise the strength of the rivets. A small sample of rivets has been rescued from the ocean bed where the wreck lies and these show a higher than expected proportion of slag in the rivets, suggesting that some of them at least are not of top quality which would make them less resistant to the impact of a collision.

The damage caused was not a long, continuous slash, which would probably have sunk the ship much quicker. It had long been assumed that this was the case, as if only a catastrophic hull failure could sink such a vessel. But in reality there was only a series of small holes in the side of the ship, totalling little more than 12 feet square in total. The sea did not come pouring through in a rush but in several places was more like water coming out of a series of fire hoses. But most importantly it affected a number of the watertight compartments and this was enough to doom the *Titanic*.

Intriguingly Barrett later testified to the British Inquiry that here was the bunker where coal had caught alight before the ship started her voyage. As a result of this, it had been emptied though not until it had burned for days. Barrett could see that it had dented the watertight compartment that was adjacent to it though it was not obvious to him whether or not this was contributing to the rate at which water was coming into the next compartment. Leading Fireman Hendrickson had been one of those responsible for getting all the coal out of the bunker. He could see when he was finished that the bulkhead next to it was dented and some of the paint on it had been scorched off.

Further back Fireman George Cavell was in another bunker shovelling coal. When the shock came, the coal in the bunker came tumbling down on top of him and he only escaped with difficulty. He heard the warning bell ringing, telling him that the watertight doors were about to clamp shut. Then the lights in his stokehold went out. It must have been terrifying but Cavell managed to fumble his way up onto deck where one of his mates told him that they had struck a berg. He later went back to draw the fires in the boiler room. When he got there, there was no water in it and he started to dampen the fires. However, they had to abandon this with the task uncompleted as the water started to come in over the floor plates. By the time they left, the water was up to their knees.

Daniel Buckley was in a cabin deep down in the ship forward, along with all the other third-class single men. He was quartered with three others in his cosy cabin. Like many in his situation, he had decided to go to America to 'make some money'. Unlike those higher up in the ship, he heard a 'terrible noise' when the ship struck the berg. However, he did not get up at once. When he did a short time later, he had a shock; his feet were wet as a trickle of water was running into the room. He tried to rouse his room-mates but they were having none of it; 'get back into bed. You are not in Ireland now', was the response.

The crew had easy access to an open area forward and they took advantage of it to see what had happened. Going out into the freezing air, they saw the small globules of ice on the deck. Some of them took them back inside to show their shipmates the evidence that they had sailed close to a berg. This was how Seaman Frank Evans first knew of the accident when one of his shipmates came in with a lump of ice from the forecastle.

Joseph Scarrott was having a cigarette when the ship struck. He was standing around the forecastle and therefore had a grandstand view of events. The collision shook the liner from stem to stern but was not as violent as might have been expected, reflecting the fact that she had struck a glancing blow. The ship shook as if the engines had been put full astern, which indeed they had been. Scarrott ran down the ladder to tell his mates what he had seen, an iceberg about the height of the Boat Deck which reminded him in shape of the Rock of Gibraltar. The crew turned out to see what was happening, getting out of their bunks and going up on deck.

But even down below there were many who were initially unaware of the serious nature of the situation. Boatswain's mate Albert Haines had good reason to celebrate the religious conventions of the time. Normally at night he would have been scrubbing the decks along with Seaman Brice but because it was a Sunday they were excused duty. Soon after the collision, Haynes heard air coming out of and water going into the forepeak. He reported to Chief Officer Wilde that the water was coming in and was told in reply to go and get all the men from his area up from down below.

Although he was disturbed by the collision, Steward Charles Andrews went back to bed but got up again when he heard the sounds of water. Mistaken impressions that the accident was not serious were quickly being put right. On the bridge, Captain Smith ordered the carpenter to go and sound the ship to find out how badly she was damaged. Chief Steward John Hardy was sent around to shut some of the upper watertight doors; only those lower down were automatically closed from the bridge.

Down the dim corridors a few hand-picked men made their way towards the bottom of the ship, to ascertain how bad the damage was and whether the watertight doors and the pumps combined would keep the ship afloat. It was time now to gather the evidence and reach a rapid conclusion about what would happen next. When the evidence was put together, no one could quite believe how dreadful the conclusion emerging from it would be.

2

A Troubled Silence

23.41–24.00, 14 April 1912

It was easy to believe at first that there was nothing to worry about. This was no instantaneous catastrophe. When the *Empress of Ireland* went down in 1914 with the loss of over 1,000, it sank fourteen minutes after being hit by another ship. The year after, the *Lusitania* went down eighteen minutes after being struck by a torpedo. In both instances, it was almost immediately obvious that the vessel would sink. Not so with *Titanic*, where the awful realization of the extent of the disaster dawned slowly, almost imperceptibly. This was would be no instant death but a long, lingering demise, almost as if it were happening in slow motion.

Major Peuchen had gone out on deck to have a look around. He saw a thin layer of light ice in the forecastle area. However, there was no sign of any imminent catastrophe. He went to tell his friend Hugo Ross that 'it was not serious; we have only struck an iceberg'. Shortly afterwards he was bringing other acquaintances forward so that they could have a look at the ice too. But then Peuchen noticed that the ship had started to list and that started to worry him. His friend Mr Hays reassured him that, as a minimum, the ship was good for another eight to ten hours.

Lawrence Beesley had been reading in his bed. All he heard was the continuing murmuring of stewards. Then the ship slowed and stopped and the vibration that was somehow a comfort disappeared. This was the first sign to him that something might be wrong. He equated it to being in a room with a loud clock; while it was ticking, one was unaware of its presence but the minute it stopped, the noise was missed. So too with *Titanic*'s reassuring vibration.

He too theorized that perhaps a propeller blade had been dropped, an accursed nuisance as it might well mean a trip back to Belfast for repairs. He jumped out of bed and donned a dressing-gown over his pyjamas. Then he put on his shoes and made his way to the hallway near the saloon. There was a steward there and Beesley asked him why the ship had stopped. The reply was a reassuring one: 'I don't know sir but I don't suppose it is anything much.'

He then climbed three flights of stairs and walked out onto the deck. The freezing night air cut him to the bone. He looked over the side into the black night but there was no sign of anything there to alarm him, certainly no iceberg looming threateningly out of the darkness. There were just two or three other people idling around there, none of whom knew of anything to worry about.

He looked through the windows of the smoking room and saw a small card school continuing to play as if nothing had happened. One of them said that he had seen an iceberg looming above the ship through the window and they had certainly felt more of a sensation than Beesley had. They guessed that the berg was about 90 feet high. But it made so little impression on the card-players that they returned to their game virtually without a break. One of them laughingly suggested that it had probably caused some damage by scraping off the new paint. This group of passengers was certainly not at all bothered. One even suggested that someone should go out and fetch a cube of ice for his whisky. This was enough for Beesley. Joining in the laughter, he then made his way back below decks and returned to his cabin to read.

The engines had stopped almost at once. To Jack Thayer, the quietness and stillness of the ship was extremely disconcerting after four and a half days of her hypnotizing vibrations. All he could hear was the breeze blowing in through his open window. Then he heard the sound of running feet and muffled voices as people hurried past in the corridor trying to find out what had occurred. He did not bother to get dressed but just put on his slippers and threw on an overcoat before venturing out.

His father decided he would join him. They made their way up to the deck. The intense darkness meant that they could see next to nothing when they looked over the rail. However, when young Jack looked forward he saw ice scattered across the forecastle in small chunks. There were just two or three others around when Thayer Senior and Junior arrived there (young Jack was first, hurrying up while his father was dressing) but they were soon joined by a number of others. They eventually found a member of the crew, who told them that they had hit an iceberg. He tried to point it out to the Thayers but they could not see it in the darkness.

After a few minutes the ship started up again but then chugged to a halt once more, this time for good. Greaser Frederick Scott was down below in the engine rooms so was better placed than most to know what happened. He thought that the ship went slow ahead for ten minutes and then slow astern for five. Quartermaster Alfred Olliver also noticed that the ship went half-speed ahead for a short time and then stopped. Situated where they were, the Collyers could hear the coughing and spluttering of the engines clearly. They were not alarmed. Harvey reassured Charlotte that there had been a slight accident in the engine room and he did not even propose to go and investigate further.

However, he then decided that he should after all try and find out more information. Charlotte and little Madge nearly fell asleep again. However, just as she was about to drop off, Harvey came back into the room and woke Charlotte up once more. 'What do you think?' he asked excitedly. 'We have struck an iceberg, a big one, but there is no danger, an officer just told me so.'

Harvey told her that the collision did not appear to have disturbed many people and there were only a few inquisitive souls up on deck. He said that he too had passed a card game in full swing. Their cards had been thrown off the table when the ship struck but they had been so little disturbed by this that they had quickly resumed their game again.

After the collision, Colonel Gracie had dressed hurriedly and then went up to the Boat Deck. He found only one other person there, a young lad. It was a beautiful night, cloudless, with the stars shining brightly. However there was no sign of any ice or icebergs. At this stage he had no idea that it was an iceberg that had been hit. He vaulted over the gate into a second-class area. He expected to be challenged by the ship's officers but saw none. This was a situation that would change later on, especially when third-class passengers were trying to get up to the Boat Deck.

Gracie crossed over onto the port side onto A Deck but could still see nothing wrong. Here he saw Bruce Ismay, effectively White Star's senior official, who wore a day suit and was hatless, as he normally was. 'He seemed too much preoccupied to notice anyone,' Gracie recalled. At the foot of the stairs he met a number of other people gathering including his great friend 'Clinch' Smith. Smith showed him a small sliver of ice, which he suggested Gracie should keep as a souvenir.

It was here that Gracie heard for the first time what had happened. The story came from someone who had been in the Smoking Room when the ship struck. He had rushed out to see what it was and came back to tell of an iceberg '50 feet' higher than the ship. Gracie also heard that the mailroom was already filling with water and the clerks were working stoically in 2 feet of it. They were transferring the mail to higher decks where they hoped it would be safe.

Elizabeth Shute was not aware of any confusion or noise of any kind at this stage. The stewardess came and told them she had learned nothing from the investigations she had carried out as to what had happened to the ship. Along the corridor, heads were peeping out of open stateroom doors, trying to find out what was going on. The atmosphere was, as Miss Shute significantly described it, 'sepulchrally still'.

Now the Graham family, which she was accompanying, and Miss Shute were all dressed. Margaret Graham, nineteen years of age, was nibbling at a chicken sandwich but was clearly unnerved by what had happened; the meat kept falling from the sandwich as her hands were shaking so much. Her tension infected Miss Shute too. For the first time she was frightened at the situation, more perhaps because of the uncertainty than any specific dread.

Going out into the corridor Miss Shute saw an officer passing. She asked him if there were anything wrong but he reassured her that he knew of nothing. However, his calm demeanour did not put her at ease for she heard him enter a cabin further down the corridor and tell someone inside, *sotto voce*, that 'we can keep the water out for a while'. Realizing that the situation might indeed be grave, Miss Shute hurried back in to put on some more clothes: a coat and skirt, slippers (quicker to put on than shoes) and a lifebelt which the stewardess helped to fit.

Eavesdropping was a good way of finding out what was going on. Dr Washington Dodge, a first-class passenger, went out and heard someone say that the ship had stopped as she had struck some ice. When someone questioned this, the man who had made the statement boldly suggested that he should go and look at the forecastle and see for himself, as it was covered in fragments of ice.

Dodge went out, strolled along the promenade and looked down on to the deck below. There he saw a large amount of ice debris, amounting in total to several cartloads worth he guessed.

It was while he was standing here that Dodge overheard a conversation that for the first time alerted him to the seriousness of the situation. Two stokers were engaged in a discussion. One asked the other (addressing him as 'sir', it was presumably a more senior member of the crew that he was talking to) if the collision had been serious. The reply put the onus back on the questioner; it was suggested that he should know better than anyone if the ship was badly damaged as he had just come up from below decks and would have better information than most onboard as to whether she had sprung any leaks or not.

The stoker, who had asked the question in the first place, remarked that 'the water was pouring into the stoke 'old when we came up, sir'. It was not a reassuring exchange to overhear. Dodge looked out over the rails and could see no ice or bergs. However, some of the steerage passengers were amusing themselves engaging in a surreal game of football played with chunks of ice. Dodge pondered on what he had heard and realized that this could be a rather tight corner to be in.

In the meantime, on the *Californian*, Third Officer Charles Groves continued to ponder on the ship he could see nearby. Groves was sure that she was 'a passenger steamer' with 'a lot of light'. Lord disagreed but Groves was insistent. He said: 'It is, sir. When she stopped her lights seemed to go out, and I suppose that they have been put out for the night.' He thought that the ship had stopped at 11.40 p.m. The British Inquiry would seize on this as the time that the *Titanic* hit the berg. They intimated that what appeared to be the lights being put out for the night might instead be the *Titanic* making a sharp turn to avoid something.

There were just two problems with this apparently incriminatory evidence. Firstly, there was the issue of the ships' times. There is much debate about what the time difference between the two ships was. Time at sea is a complex subject but the basic premise is that ships sailing west set their clocks based on the next day's noon position. There are different views of what the time difference between *Titanic* and *Californian* was. Some suggest that the *Californian* was twelve minutes behind the *Titanic*, others that she was seventeen minutes ahead. Therefore, it is impossible to state with confidence that the time at which Stone saw the lights go out was the same time that the *Titanic* swerved to miss an iceberg.

The second issue is a much more basic one. Groves said that he had a conversation with Captain Lord debating whether or not they were looking at a passenger steamer. Lord had no recollection of such a conversation ever taking place. It would be something of a habit; Groves was one of just three officers on the *Californian* who would later claim that they had had a conversation with their captain at some stage that night which he could not recall, the other two being Second Officer Stone and Apprentice Gibson.

Back on the *Titanic*, after returning to his room following his initial foray out to see what had happened, Second Office Lightoller now lay snugly in his bed. He felt he should do something but reasoned that, if he were needed, someone would surely come and get him. It was about ten minutes after the collision when there was a knock on his door. It was Boxhall, who told him quietly that there was something wrong. Lightoller responded that he already knew there was. Then Boxhall told him of the collision with the ice. The ship had been pierced and water was now in the mail room on F Deck. Then he left. Lightoller got dressed and went out on deck to try and make himself useful.

The impact had awoken Bruce Ismay but he had stayed in bed for a short time. He then went out into the corridor to see what was going on. He asked a steward but he had little information so Ismay put a coat on and went up on deck. He went to see the Captain, who told him that they had struck ice. He then sought out the Chief Engineer who felt that the blow had been a serious one but that the pumps would be able to keep the water out. Such confidence would soon start to evaporate.

It can only have been a few minutes after the berg was struck that Smith came into the wireless shack, as he still had not received the results of the inspection into the damage that he had ordered. He told Phillips and Bride, the wireless operators, that the ship had struck a berg and that they should make themselves ready to send a call for assistance. However, they should hang on until he knew more.

Thomas Andrews then came on the bridge to see Captain Smith. He and the carpenter then took a backstairs tour of the Titanic to inspect the damage. It soon became clear that it was terminal. She was designed so that any two of her compartments might be flooded and she would stay afloat. Even the first four watertight compartments could be breached but she would still not sink. She would be at a pretty uncomfortable angle it was true but she would at least have remained on the surface. But the way in which she had hit the ice had allowed water into six compartments; too many for the ship to live. Andrews made his way back to the bridge with his awful and unbelievable news.

A terrifying picture started to emerge, though at this stage only a few people were aware of it. On the bridge, Captain Smith had quickly taken steps to ascertain the full extent of the damage. As well as Andrews, Fourth Officer Boxhall had been sent below to try and find out how serious the damage done to the ship was. Initially, he could find none – he must have been looking in the wrong place. When he reported back to Captain Smith, he was asked to go and find the ship's carpenter. However, it was the carpenter who found Boxhall and told him that *Titanic* had been holed and was taking on water fast. While the carpenter made his way to the Captain to make his report, Boxhall continued to journey down into the bowels of the ship.

He arrived at the Post Room, where the mail clerks were working frantically – they had about 400,000 items of mail to worry about. The lowest deck, where the post was stored, was already virtually flooded with water within 2 feet of the deck on which Boxhall was now standing. He could clearly see mailbags floating. There was no doubt that there had been serious damage and Boxhall hurried back to Captain Smith to tell him the bad news as soon as possible.

First-class passenger Norman Chambers had also gone down to investigate. He saw some mailmen who had come up from the Post Room who were wet through. Looking down he could see that the water level was up to within 18 inches of the next deck. He could see letters floating on the surface. He was not though especially alarmed and made a joke of it. He was confident that *Titanic*'s watertight compartmentalization would more than cope with any problems.

It was the crew and third-class passengers far below who realized that there were serious problems first, probably even before those in command on the bridge. Those of the crew who were up on deck noticed a large amount of ice and snow on the starboard deck. However, it did not seem to have been a serious collision so most of them trooped down again, cursing the situation more for the fact that it had disturbed their sleep than for any sense of danger they felt. They had not been back in their cabins long though before the boatswain came in and told them all to get up and help in uncovering the boats.

Some down below heard evidence of problems before they actually saw it. Able Seaman Edward Buley was quartered with some of his colleagues in the front of the ship. They noticed the sound of water coming in although they could not yet see anything. There was a hatchway in the forecastle with a tarpaulin across it. Water could be heard rushing in below it.

Seaman Samuel Hemming also heard the 'hissing noise' of the air escaping from the forepeak. He had not been too disturbed at the time of the collision and had gone back to his bunk after getting up to investigate. He was soon shaken from his lethargy, when the boatswain came in and said, 'turn out, you fellows, you haven't half an hour to live. That is from Mr Andrews. Keep it to yourself and let no one know.' It was about midnight now and even at this early stage it seems that those in authority already knew that the ship was doomed. However, they seemed surprisingly lax in appraising some others of the fact, especially those responsible for loading the lifeboats soon afterwards.

Steward Joseph Wheat was quartered on F Deck next to the Turkish baths. He was awoken by the collision. He woke his room-mate and then went out to find out what had happened. He found out that the ship had been holed and that water was coming in forward. He then went down to the Post Room on G Deck where he too saw the staff moving the post bags up from the rising water. He also saw water already starting to creep up the stairs. He then saw it to start to slowly cover G Deck where he was standing.

He then went up to manually close the watertight doors by the Turkish baths (only the watertight doors down in the lowest areas of the ship were closed automatically from the bridge). There were in fact two there. One he managed to close himself, the other had to be closed from above (E Deck) and he had help to shut that one. It helped delay the spread of the water but nothing more. The way that the bulkheads had been constructed meant that they did not go up high enough and water would inevitably tip over from one compartment to the next as the forward sections of the ship dipped down into the water. It was perhaps significant that it was not Wheat's job to close these watertight doors and he did so on his own initiative.

In order for the *Titanic* to stay afloat for as long as possible there had to be a system in place for closing the doors manually and it is not clear that there was any such thing in operation.

Now aware that his ship was in real trouble, Captain Smith re-entered the wireless shack about ten minutes after his first visit and asked Phillips to send out a message for assistance. The recently held Berlin Convention had decided on a new code, 'SOS', as the standard international distress code. It was about to make its debut. In the meantime, Boxhall worked out the position of the ship for transmission to other ships. As it was night he could not take a position and had to rely on 'dead reckoning'. This was a process by which the ship's last known position was taken as a starting point and a new position calculated by taking her speed and bearing since then.

Unfortunately, for whatever reason Boxhall calculated a position that was significantly wrong. This was not known at the time but was confirmed when the wreck was discovered in 1985. There was however plenty of evidence for those who cared to look at it with an open mind that the position was obviously wrong even in 1912. It did not make much difference to those aboard the *Titanic* that night, though it might have done.

It was now time to start getting the passengers up on deck. There must be no panic. Perhaps the wireless operators might pick up a ship close at hand. The chances of passenger survival would be made better if those aboard could be encouraged to stay calm. However, it was time to start taking precautionary measures just in case. This would be the job of the stewards.

The approach taken was contingent on what class a passenger happened to be in. In first-class, Steward Henry Etches went to look after his charges, a small, select group including Benjamin Guggenheim. He helped Guggenheim and his secretary dress in their lifebelts, taking them out of the wardrobe where they were stored and putting them on. Guggenheim did not think much of them. The stewards responsible for second- and third-class had large numbers of people to look after and just flung open doors and told those in the cabins to get up and put lifebelts on.

But still at this stage for most people there was no sense of panic or urgency. Paul Maugé, who worked in the *a la carte* restaurant, poked his head out of the door but was told by a steward 'there is no danger, it is better that you go to sleep'. There was little sign of imminent disaster and most people aboard still assumed that there was nothing to worry about. The immediate emotion of most people was curiosity rather than fear. Hardly anyone on the *Titanic* had any idea that the ship had just over two hours to live. And those who did know were generally not letting on.

3

Uncovering the Boats

00.01–00.30, 15 April 1912

Armed with the still fairly private knowledge that the maiden voyage of the world's largest ship was transforming itself into a nightmare of Dante-esque proportions, Captain Smith now had to face the unthinkable. There were twenty boats located on the Boat Deck and they needed to be prepared for use. With over 2,200 souls onboard they also needed to be prepared mentally to use them. They somehow had to be persuaded to leave the largest ship in the world and be lowered 70 feet onto the vast North Atlantic in comparatively tiny lifeboats. This would be no easy task. Everything must be done quietly, in an orderly fashion. Nevertheless, it was now time to uncover the boats.

However, there were some practical issues making the situation even worse than it already was. Four of the boats were collapsibles with sides that had to be pulled up before they were lowered. Two of these were readily accessible on the deck area, the idea being that when the ordinary lifeboats next to them had been lowered away, they could be fitted in the davits and filled too. However, the two stowed on top of the Officer's Cabin would be very difficult to get down onto the Boat Deck, weighing several tons each as they did.

In addition, the lack of a meaningful boat drill was also about to show itself as a critical problem. There had been no instructions issued to the passengers as to which lifeboat they would use in a time of emergency; how could there be when there were not enough lifeboats to go around? It was little better with the crew either. On the Friday before, lists had gone up detailing members of the crew to various lifeboat stations but not everyone seems to have read them or even known of their existence. Even those who did sometimes chose to ignore it on this particular night. And by definition, as only sixteen men had taken part in the cursory lifeboat drill at Southampton, some of them would not even have had a practice at rowing a boat. Indeed, it would later emerge that some of them had never rowed a boat before, full stop.

There was a further problem, one that was effectively a death sentence for nearly 500 people aboard who might otherwise have been saved. It revolved around the so-called 'lowering capacity' of lifeboats, that is how many people could safely be lowered in the boats as opposed to be on them when they were afloat on the water. Second Officer Lightoller epitomized the issue. He had been onboard both when the lifeboats had been tested in the trials in Belfast and also when the boat drill had been held in Southampton but he had never seen a lifeboat filled to anything like its full capacity. He therefore believed there was a risk that, if too many people were put on the boats before they were lowered, then the ropes lowering them would break or the boats might buckle with disastrous results. Such was not the case but Lightoller believed it was, and he would be responsible for supervising the lowering of the boats on the port side.

There was therefore no such thing as a formal drill for loading the boats in place. Lightoller contrasted the Merchant Navy with the more disciplined approach of the Royal Navy. He explained it away by saying that in the Merchant Navy men were expected to show initiative. In his later justification of the lack of formal organization, he was to reveal much about the amateurish nature of the way in which the ship was run. It seemed as if the maxim was for every man to make his own decisions.

Rather than formal organization, it was a case of the officers aboard making it up as they went along. But, to use another cliché, everything would not be alright on this particular night. Instinct, which the Second Officer claimed was the best thing to follow in such situations, would not be sufficient. Lightoller would later claim that the loading of the boats that night went off without a hitch. On an occasion where myths soon began to overlay reality, this would turn out to be one of the more unjustified interpretations of events.

Organization was made more difficult by the noise of steam blowing off through the exhausts now that the engines had been stopped. The sound of this was deafening and officers could barely make themselves heard above the din. The seamen came pouring out on deck. It was too noisy to tell them what to do so hand signals had to suffice for directing them. The boats were uncovered, an act with an ominous symbolism with the *Titanic* alone in the cold, dark sea.

Large numbers of passengers were appearing, their faces understandably etched with fear. Lightoller tried to reassure them with a smile but, even as the covers were taken off the boats, he was aware that the ship was starting to settle. Soon the Bosun's Mate, whom Lightoller had delegated with the task of uncovering the boats, came over to report to him that the job was done. The Second Officer nodded in recognition and intimated that it was time for the boats to be swung out.

As Lightoller prepared the boats, he noticed Bruce Ismay round about. After those fateful discussions with Captain Smith and Andrews on the bridge which confirmed the imminent fate of the *Titanic*, Ismay had gone back to his room, presumably to get some warmer clothes on, and then back up onto the bridge. Here he heard the Captain giving an order to the crew about the loading of boats. He went to the Boat Deck and spoke to one of the officers there (perhaps Pitman) about loading them up. He admitted freely that he started to give orders to the officers: 'I met one of the officers. I told him to get the boat out …' though he did not recall which officer it was. Then, in his words, he rendered all the assistance he could in putting the women and children in. Throughout it all, he noticed no signs of panic on deck.

In the meantime, some of the passengers had noticed a strangeness about the ship and the way she was sitting in the water. 'Clinch' Smith and Colonel Gracie had by now noticed a list. They did not mention it to any others as they did not wish to alarm them. Smith and Gracie resolved to stay together if a crisis ensued. Gracie pictured the two of them on a raft with no food or water. The two of them went back to their staterooms to prepare themselves for the ordeal ahead. Gracie packed his three large travelling bags so that they could be transferred to another ship should the need arrive. The raft still appeared a very distant possibility.

As he moved through the ship he saw stewards assisting men and women into their lifejackets. Steward Charles Cullen came up to Gracie and helped him to put his on. Returning to A Deck on the port side towards the stern Gracie found the unprotected ladies he had formed an acquaintance with during the trip. These were

Mrs Charlotte Appleton, wife of an old school-friend, Mrs Malvina Cornell, wife of a New York judge, and Mrs Caroline Brown, wife of a Boston publisher. They were all sisters, returning home from the funeral of their sibling, Lady Victor Drummond. Also there was Miss Edith Evans, their friend; Gracie had not been introduced to her before and did not yet know her by name.

The Strauses were present too, along with Mr and Mrs Astor, as well as Hugh Woolner, son of a famous English sculptor and H. Björnström Steffanson, a young Swedish army lieutenant; he knew Gracie's wife's relatives back in Sweden. Soon the band began to play. The songs they played were cheerful and not hymns. Gracie was certain that they never played 'Nearer My God to Thee' and later said he would have made a point of noting if they had done so as a particularly inappropriate, even morbid, selection in light of the possible fate that was beginning to loom, hardly calculated to calm the nerves of those aboard.

Jack Thayer had quite early on noticed a list to port (the original list had been to starboard, and presumably changed as successive 'watertight' compartments were filled) and also felt that the ship was distinctly down by the head. After going outside to investigate, the bitter night air forced the Thayers, father and son, back inside into the warmth of one of the lounges. There was a fair crowd gathered now, dazed and unsure what was happening. Just then, Bruce Ismay and Thomas Andrews passed. Knowing Andrews on a social basis, the Thayers asked him what the problem was. He replied quietly that he did not believe that the ship had much more than an hour to live.

It was around 12.15 a.m., that the stewards passed the word around that everyone was to put on their lifebelts. By the time that the Thayers returned to their staterooms, both Mrs Thayer and her maid were fully dressed. Young Jack put on some clothes; a green tweed suit and several jumpers along with his coat. He put on his cork lifejacket and then his overcoat on top. He had after all been outside for the past half an hour and he knew better than most exactly how freezing the night air was.

He then returned to A Deck which was now getting very busy. He bumped into his new-found acquaintance Milton Long and they decided to stick together. There was a great deal of noise by now. The band was doing their best to give a surreal semblance of normality by playing lively numbers but nobody was listening to them. Jack and Long went out on deck and found the boats ready to launch. This was clearly a serious situation but there was as yet no sense of panic or crisis.

Amazingly, onboard the stricken ship the routine of ship life still went on. Lookout George Hogg and his mate still took over from Fleet and Lee at 12.23 a.m. ('old' *Titanic* time which was due to change to midnight to keep the clocks aligned with their longitude). Of course, they might have been invaluable now as they eyes of the ship picking up signs of other ships in the area. It is interesting, perhaps one might think crucial in terms of later allegations against the *Californian*, that they saw no other ship from their lofty eyrie. However, the lookouts, in common with most other crew members, did not seem aware of how serious the situation was. A while later, when Hogg saw people milling around on the decks with lifebelts on, he phoned the bridge to ask if they were still needed in the crowsnest but got no reply.

Down below, Lawrence Beesley was aware of the volume of voices outside his cabin increasing and thought that he should go out and find out what was happening. He decided to dress this time, putting on a thick Norfolk jacket and trousers and then making his way up to the deck. More people were up there now, asking each other what had happened, unaware of any specific problems. The night was so cold that he walked up and down merely to keep warm.

He decided to go down again but as he did so, he passed an officer. He watched as he moved across to Boat 16 and took the cover off. No one seemed to bother too much about this and neither was there any sign of any concern, let alone panic, among the passengers milling around. Yet as he looked down the deck Beesley was sure he saw a tilting downwards towards the bows, as if the ship were listing. It was a sensation that was exaggerated when he walked down the stairs, which seemed to him to be throwing him forwards.

Back on D Deck, where his cabin was situated, he met three ladies engaged in conversation. They asked him why they had stopped, to which Beesley replied that they were now moving again. However, when they insisted that the throb of the engines was absent, he took them to a bathroom and, when they placed their hands on the bath, they could still feel that reassuring vibration (an interesting story this, confirming indeed that the ship's engines did restart for a short time though perhaps slightly later than some suggested). He then went back to his cabin again, passing unconcerned stewards in the corridors as he went.

In his corridor, he met another man, getting dressed and putting a tie on. The stranger laughingly told him to peep in and look at his neighbour. In the top bunk of the room was a man, wrapped up in bed, telling the unwelcome intruders that if they thought he was going out on a freezing deck on a night like this, then they had another thing coming. Beesley returned once more to his room and put on some underclothes. After a gap of about ten minutes, he heard a steward pacing the corridor, shouting: 'All passengers on deck with lifebelts on!'

Beesley put on his lifebelt and started to walk up towards the upper decks but was stopped by a lady who said that she had no lifebelt. He took her back down to F Deck where her cabin was and a steward found it for her. Once more climbing towards the deck, he passed the Purser's office and heard the clanging of a door inside; the Purser, he felt sure, was emptying the safe of some of its more valuable items.

Returning to the top deck, there were a considerable number of people there now. Some were fully dressed, prepared for a cold night, but others seemed to have just thrown on whatever was at hand at the time that might be warm. The ship had stopped again and there was virtually no motion. Looking over the side into the darkness, the water seemed even further below than it actually was. To Beesley, the ship felt like a rock. Onboard, on the top decks at least, all was calm and quiet. Passengers kept out of the way and said little, though the noise of steam escaping from the exhausts was so deafening that they could not have heard each other anyway.

Passengers were still pouring up now (Beesley estimated the time as being about 12.20 a.m.). The crew were working on the lifeboats and, as the crowd watched, the crank-handles on the davits were turned and the boats started to lift and then move towards the side of the Boat Deck. Women and children were then ordered down to the deck below and men to stay where they were. Several women refused to leave their husbands but were persuaded to do so. The separation of women and men started to impress upon some of those present that the situation was perhaps more concerning than they had thought.

Major Peuchen, sensing trouble, had gone to his room to get some heavy clothes on. When he came up towards the Boat Deck, he saw a number of people congregated around the top of the Grand Staircase. Several of the ladies, he noticed, were crying. Mrs Anna Warren, a first-class passenger, had gone back to her room and put on some warm clothes. She and some friends went to the foot of the Grand

Staircase on D Deck. As they were there, Mr Andrews rushed by, going up the stairs. When asked if there was any danger, he made no reply. However, another passenger noticed a look of terror in his face. Not long after word arrived that the squash courts were underwater, as was the baggage hold. The forward part of the ship was starting to fill.

The Collyers had been about to turn in again when the sound of quite a few people passing the cabin disturbed Charlotte. The noise they made reminded her of rats running through an empty room. She looked at herself in the mirror and was shocked at how white her face was. She put a dressing gown on over her nightdress and tied her hair up with a ribbon. She noticed that the ship appeared to be tilting slightly as she wrapped Madge up in a blanket. No valuables were picked up for everyone thought they would be back in the room soon, but they now made their way up to the open deck.

Being disturbed, Margaret Brown looked out into the corridor. She saw a man, pale with fright, who told her to get her lifebelt on. He was a buyer from Gimbel Brothers, a company based in Paris and New York. She put her lifebelt on and dressed in her furs. She then made her way up to the A deck where she saw Mrs Bucknell again who reminded her of their premonitory conversation earlier that evening. Some still made light of the situation. Mrs Vera Dick, from Calgary, Canada, was told to put on her lifebelt by a man who told her that 'they are the latest thing this season'.

Others however were shaken from any complacency in the most alarming way. Mrs J. B. Mennell (her married name in Gracie's book; at the time of the disaster she was unmarried Elizabeth Allen) was told by the maid of her aunt that the baggage room was full of water. She replied that she should not worry, as the watertight doors would have been closed and she should go back to her cabin. When she got there (it was on E Deck) it was already filling with water.

Far down below, on *Titanic*'s lower decks, the stewards were getting their passengers up and dressed. Steward George Crowe was quartered amidships on the lower deck. When he got up, he saw lots of stewards and steerage passengers moving from forward (where the single male steerage quarters were) to aft. Daniel Buckley heard the stewards going along the corridor, shouting: 'All up on deck! Unless you want to get drowned.'

Buckley made his way to the upper decks with no problem but when he got there he noticed that he did not have a lifebelt when

most others did. He went down below to get it but when he returned
to the lower decks the water had already risen up four steps. When
he arrived back on the lower deck, there were still a number of his
fellow passengers down there. The girls, he noted, were excitable and
in tears, with the men trying to console them.

Buckley was one of the few third-class survivors to testify at the
US Inquiry (better at least than the British equivalent, which did
not bother calling any). He was an uncomfortable and sometimes
contradictory witness who did not seem to want to metaphorically
rock the boat. For example, he said that he was not aware of any
attempts to prevent steerage from going up to the boats, but then
immediately contradicted himself by saying: 'they tried to keep us
down at first on the steerage deck. They did not want us to go up to
the first-class place at all'.

However, there is perhaps an explanation for this apparent
contradiction. The most likely scenario is that steerage were not kept,
like rats waiting to drown, below decks but they were required on
the whole to stay in their own above-deck areas and not permitted to
trespass into first-class areas. In ordinary circumstances, this would
just have reflected the social apartheid of the time. However, in the
current case it was a matter of life and death because the Boat Deck
was mainly in a first-class area. Therefore, there was discrimination
against third-class in favour of both first and second-class, just
because of where the boats were.

Buckley corroborates this interpretation when he witnessed such
a case of segregation going on. He saw one of the *Titanic*'s sailors
throw a steerage passenger back over 'a little gate'. This was the barrier
between the top of some stairs from down below and the first-class
deck. The sailor then locked it but the steerage passenger was furious.
He broke the lock and chased after the seaman. The irate passenger
did not seem as bothered by escaping as by his desire to catch the
errant sailor, saying that if he caught him he 'would throw him in
the water'. This was the opening that many steerage passengers were
waiting for. After that Buckley noted 'they could not keep them down'.

However, below decks was a rabbit-warren and passengers who did
not know their way around might find themselves trapped in a *cul
de sac*, literally a dead end. Only one man seems to have done much
about this problem, which affected third-class passengers almost
exclusively given their location on the ship. His name was Steward
John Hart. About three quarters of an hour after the collision, Hart

took third-class women and children from third-class to the first-class companionway. He had been given orders to take them to the Boat Deck. It would however take him a long time to get there.

Certainly water was by now pouring into the forward parts of the ship. Able Seaman John Poingdestre had gone back to his quarters to pick up his boots – he reckoned that this was about three quarters of an hour after the collision. He was coming out again when a wooden bulkhead (not a watertight compartment) separating his quarters from third-class suddenly collapsed and water came cascading in. As he made his way back he noticed a large number of third-class passengers from forward along with their luggage. They had escaped from the corridor below but were only in the open area behind the forecastle, still a long way from the Boat Deck.

At some stage some of the firemen and engineers had returned to the engine rooms in an attempt to man the pumps. One of them was trimmer Thomas Dillon. In order to allow the men down below to move around more easily some of the watertight doors were re-opened by hand. Dillon did not remember them ever being shut again.

Titanic's main hope now lay in any ships that might be close at hand that could come to the rescue. This put a huge onus on the ship's wireless operators. The call for help had gone out – 'CQD', the old call, first of all. Bride had laughingly suggested that they should send out the new call, 'SOS', as it might be the last chance they ever had to use it. Captain Smith told him that the berg had struck amidships. The wireless operators (or specifically Phillips, as there was only one set of apparatus) had immediately sent out the message.

Bride, however, does not always come across as a reliable witness and his evidence, certainly for a *New York Times* interview that he gave later, should be treated with a liberal pinch of salt. For example, he stated in this that Phillips had seen the iceberg ten minutes before they struck it. It is not clear how he had done this when Fleet had only seen it from the crows-nest about forty seconds before the ship hit it.

Responses to the messages soon came in. The first was from the *Frankfurt*. Their wireless operator went off to tell his captain the unbelievable news that the new super-liner had struck a berg and was in urgent need of help. By the time he came back across the ether, Bride could already feel the ship starting to sink by the head. Bride, whose job during the time that followed appeared to be the important one of 'go-between' for Phillips whereby he would keep the Captain informed of developments as they emerged, took it to the bridge.

Other messages went out across the waves urging help. On the *Virginian*, the operator was simply not believed at first by the Officer on watch. He was being dismissed from the bridge with a flea in his ear for his warped sense of humour when he kicked the captain's door (he had turned in for the night) and woke him. Only when his report was delivered to the captain in person was he believed and the ship headed in the direction of the position given in the distress call.

The boats were provisioned with food and water but not everyone seemed to know where the provisions were kept as later a number of shortages were later reported. However, they certainly did not have pre-stored lights in them. The lamps were kept in a special room and now it was the job of Samuel Hemming to fetch them and dish them out to each boat. However, he would not manage to do this for all of them.

Far down below attempts were still being made to draw the fires. Leading Fireman Charles Hendrickson had been asked by engineer John Hesketh to fetch some lamps to help light the engine rooms to do this. As he made his way down through the lower decks, he passed through crowds of third-class passengers carrying their trunks and possessions with them away from their flooding quarters. He did not take much notice of them at the time but when he later returned from down below he saw that there were still there, sitting around as if awaiting instructions.

In the meantime, some few miles away (how many was soon to become a matter of heated debate) the *Californian* still lay virtually stationary, just drifting almost imperceptibly in the current. An intriguing tale was to emerge from one of her crew members at a later stage. It came from 'donkeyman' Ernest Gill. He said that he had come up on deck at 11.56 p.m., *Californian* time. The stars were bright, it was very clear and he could see for a long distance. The ship's engines had been stopped at 10.30 p.m. and she was drifting in ice floes. Looking to starboard, he could see a 'large steamer' about 10 miles away moving at full speed. He would later tell the British Inquiry:

> It could not have been anything but a passenger boat – she was too large. I could see two rows of lights which I took to be porthole lights and several groups of lights which I took to be saloon and deck lights. I knew it was a passenger boat. That is all I saw of the ship … She was a good distance off I should say no more than 10 miles and probably less.

Captain Herbert Stone, Second Officer of the *Californian*, had come on the bridge at 12.08 a.m., *Californian* time. He also saw a steamer to the south-south-east, stopped. He saw 'one masthead light, her red sidelight [displayed on a ship's port side] and some small indistinct lights around the deck which looked like portholes or open doors. I judged her to be a small tramp steamer and about 5 miles distant.' In fact, it was Lord who briefed him about the other ship when Stone began his watch. The Captain had told him that they were stopped in the ice and he did not plan to move again before the morning. He pointed out the nearby steamer to him, noted that she was stopped and instructed Stone to tell him if the two ships should drift any closer to each other. Lord then went below to the Chart Room leaving Stone in charge of the bridge. He later recalled that it was about 12.10 a.m.

Stone replaced Groves who now also went off watch. Groves went down to the wireless shack before turning in. He fancied himself as something of an amateur wireless operator and often tried his hand with Cyril Evans guiding him. However, Evans was tired and perhaps a trifle miffed after *Titanic*'s rude rebuff just over an hour before. Groves put the headphones on but could hear nothing. He did not realize that the dynamo that drove the power supply had wound down and that there was no charge left in the apparatus. At about the same time, *Titanic*'s wireless operator Jack Phillips had started to transmit his distress signals.

Apprentice James Gibson came up on the bridge of the *Californian* at about 12.15 a.m. He shared a coffee with Stone, and Stone pointed out to him the ship on *Californian*'s starboard beam. To both of them (and to Captain Lord) it appeared to be a ship with one masthead light (though Third Officer Groves who had seen her earlier thought that she had two). As Gibson looked over, he saw a flash come from the other vessel. At first he thought it was a Morse lamp signalling and he started to Morse her back. However, when he looked through the binoculars he could see that it was not a Morse lamp messaging them at all but a flickering light.

He could also see a port side light and the faint glare of other lights on her after deck. He remarked to Stone that she looked like a tramp steamer, an assessment that the Second Officer agreed with. To Gibson, the ship he was looking at 'had no appearance at all of a passenger steamer'. At about 12.25 a.m., Gibson went below to pick up a new log. He returned soon after as he could not find it and then went off the bridge once more, this time for nearly half an hour.

So the Second Officer and the Apprentice of the *Californian* both felt that they were looking at a tramp steamer, as had Captain Lord. However, Ernest Gill believed that he had seen a passenger steamer; so too did Third Officer Groves. These were two very different sets of views. It would not be the last difference of opinion to emerge about what was seen and done onboard the *Californian* that night. The conflicting, confusing and downright contradictory story of the *Californian* incident was already being written. And, even as it was, the fate of the *Titanic* was becoming more and more certain.

4

Lower Away

00.31–01.00, 15 April 1912

Some 50 miles south of the *Titanic*, on the more southerly east-bound track and therefore well out of danger, the *Carpathia* was proceeding towards Europe unconcerned by anything other than the normal anxieties of the ship's passengers and crew. Harold Cottam was the only wireless operator onboard the *Carpathia*. Like all such technicians on such 'one-man ships' he did not work regular hours but largely decided them for himself.

The job was not very well paid (about £4 10*s* a month) but there was a certain glamour about it that attracted a significant number of young men to join up, take the training course and become an operator. His apparatus was not the best available with a normal effective range of about 250 miles, much less than that of the *Titanic* or even the *Californian* for example.

It was pure luck that Cottam was still up, as he normally turned in about midnight. Cottam was waiting for a reply from the *Parisian* to a message he had sent earlier and would otherwise have been in bed with the wireless off. There had as yet been no reply so he then switched over to the Cape Race land station to see if there was anything of interest from there, after which he planned to turn in – the reply he was waiting for was routine and not urgent. He heard a batch of mundane commercial messages from Cape Cod for the *Titanic* and decided to contact her to see if she was aware of them.

He must have been stunned when he got the reply from Phillips on the *Titanic*: 'Come at once. We have struck an iceberg. It's CQD Old Man.'

Betraying his incredulity, Cottam asked: 'Shall I tell my captain? Do you require assistance?

The answer ended any lingering doubts: 'Yes. Come quick.'

Cottam ran to the bridge, where First Officer Dean was on watch. Together they went to see Captain Rostron. The two men barged in without knocking, which irritated the very correct master, a stickler for discipline. However, he reacted in a flash when they passed on the news, though he too was shocked, asking Cottam if he was certain that his information was correct.

On receipt of this almost incredible information, Captain Rostron sparked into life. *Titanic's* distress call was received at 12.35 a.m. *Carpathia* time (Rostron recalled this was 10.45 p.m. New York time). Rostron ordered the ship to be turned around and *then* asked if the radio message was correct. Then came his orders, a meticulous list made all the more impressive as it was improvised under enormous pressure. They are worth mentioning in detail as they give a fascinating insight into the mental prowess of a sea captain of outstanding quality. They included the following provisions:

The Chief Engineer to summon another watch of stokers and make all possible speed.

The First Officer (who was currently on watch) to prepare all the lifeboats.

The English, Italian and Hungarian doctors to deal with First, Second and Third Class survivors respectively. Each doctor to have supplies of stimulants and restoratives on hand.

Rooms to be freed up to accommodate survivors. These included not only cabins but also dining rooms, smoking rooms and the library.

Pursers to be ready to receive survivors onboard and prepare a list to be sent by wireless as soon as possible.

Stewards designated to keep *Carpathia's* own passengers out of the way.

Coffee, soup, tea etc. to be made available in the saloons along with blankets.

All boats to be swung out and all gangway doors to be opened.

A chair slung at each gangway to hoist injured or infirm survivors up onto the ship.

Ladders to be made ready to hang over the side and canvas and ash bags to be made available to pull small children up.

Rockets to be prepared to be fired when they got closer to *Titanic*'s reported position to reassure those aboard her that help was on the way.

It should be borne in mind that this was not a list that Rostron had hours to think about, it is what he came up with more or less on the spur of the moment. He required that each officer delegated a task report back to him personally to confirm that it had been satisfactorily carried out. This meticulous attention to detail provides a marked and very unflattering comparison to Captain Smith's actions on the *Titanic* that night.

Rostron also differed in another important respect. He of course would have been only too well aware of the dangers of ice from the parlous position that the ship he was trying to aid was in. However, it seems clear enough from his general approach that he would have been cautious with ice around anyway. Aware of the risk he was taking, he put on extra lookouts; he had two men placed forward on the deck and one in the crow's nest. It was, he later said, always his policy to post a man forward in times of risk as they would often spot objects in front of them before the lookout in the crow's nest would.

After passing on the shock news to Rostron, Cottam returned to his post, wide awake now. A few minutes later he picked up a conversation with the *Frankfurt*. Then another message came in for the *Titanic* from her older sister, *Olympic*. The *Titanic* did not pick it up; Cottam asked the *Titanic* if she had received it and she said no, so Phillips then made contact with his opposite number on the *Olympic*.

As the reply from the *Carpathia* came in, Bride took it to Captain Smith on the bridge. It cannot have been entirely good news; Rostron's predicted arrival time of four hours later would leave *Titanic* at the bottom of the North Atlantic for a good couple of hours at least and probably more. However, it was better than nothing and maybe other ships might be raised via wireless. Clearly, Smith was concerned as he came back to the wireless shack with Bride. *Olympic* was now in communication too though she was much further away, far too far to be of any practical use.

When Bride went to tell Captain Smith of the *Carpathia*'s response, he had to push through a crush of people to do so. Then he returned to the shack, where Phillips told him to get dressed. In the excitement, Bride had forgotten that he had not done so. He went to his cabin, put on his clothes and returned with an overcoat for Phillips, as the night was icy cold. From then on, he went to the Captain's cabin every few minutes with updates.

In the meantime, the *Frankfurt* did not reply to the initial message from the *Titanic* for another twenty minutes and when she did come back her message was vague; she clearly had not understood how serious things were. However, the seriousness of the situation did not seem to have dawned yet on Jack Phillips either. Rather than exercise some patience, Phillips – by now in communication with the *Carpathia* whose operator clearly *had* grasped the full extent of the *Titanic*'s plight – told the *Frankfurt*'s operator that he was a 'fool' and to stay out of future conversations.

This was extraordinary, especially as the *Frankfurt*'s signal was so strong that the *Titanic*'s operators thought she was quite close, though as it happened she was too far away to provide practical assistance in time anyway. Another ship, the *Mount Temple*, had later been in communication with the *Frankfurt* which helped confirm her position, which was too far to the west to be of use.

At the American Inquiry that was held after the loss of the *Titanic*, Senator Smith, the Chairman, was quite rightly much disturbed at this flippant attitude on the part of the *Titanic*'s operator and suggested strongly that the sinking liner should have tried to explain her situation more patiently even if the *Frankfurt*'s operator was indeed a 'fool'; this was no time for *prima donnas*. Other ships were picked up too, such as the *Baltic*, too far off to be of assistance (about 350 miles) but informed by the *Caronia* of the *Titanic*'s precarious position anyway.

At 12.30 a.m. (ship's time) Captain James Moore, skipper of the *Mount Temple*, had been awakened with a message from the Marconi operator. It had come in from the *Titanic*; it ended 'come at once. Iceberg'. Moore went to the Chart Room, worked out the ships' relative positions and steered east. They were about 49 miles away, he calculated (though this was understated by at least 8 miles because Boxhall had worked out *Titanic*'s position incorrectly). Before setting off, he gave instructions that the 'fireman' should be woken up; if necessary, he was to be given a tot of rum to encourage him; an interesting management technique that one is unlikely to see copied in the modern world.

As the night went on, the *Mount Temple* would be a distant observer of other wireless messages sent to the *Titanic*. She picked up several from the *Olympic*, (500 miles away from the *Titanic*) asking first of all 'are you steering south to meet us', which clearly intimated that the seriousness of the situation was not at all clear to *Titanic*'s sister.

Others picked up the distress call too but were too far distant to get there in time to make a difference. Gilbert Balfour was a travelling inspector for the Marconi Company and was onboard the *Baltic* when he picked up *Titanic*'s CQD. The ship immediately turned around but was in no position to help though it did not stop her doing her best.

By the time that *Titanic*'s boats were swung out and ready to lower, the water was already nearly level with the deck at her bows. Yet revealingly Lightoller still did not think that the ship would sink. In his evidence in New York, where he generally said as little as possible, this was one question that seemed to put him on the defensive. When asked why he did not take more risks when lowering these first boats, he said emphatically: 'I did not know it was urgent then. I had no idea it was urgent.'

Here was a strange chain of events. The man tasked with lowering the lifeboats had not yet been told by his captain that his ship was going to founder. It is a shame; maybe Lightoller might have thought about putting on a few more people if he had known the grave extent of the damage that had been caused to the ship.

Lightoller had been to see the Captain to suggest that the lifeboats should be lowered with women and children loaded. Again, this is suggestive. The Second Officer suggests to the Captain what should be done, not the other way round. It seems as if Captain Smith, overwhelmed by the magnitude of the disaster which now not only loomed but was unavoidable, had retreated into a shell and left the decision-making to others. Nothing could have been more undesirable at such a time. A firm hand was needed but no one was there to provide it.

Lightoller saw Captain Smith several times during the rest of the ship's life but the Captain seems to have been surprisingly peripheral. The Second Officer would later have a vague recollection of seeing his Captain on the bridge towards the end. His last direct orders to Lightoller, given now, were to lower away women and children. However, this is not a decisive instruction but a response to Lightoller's own suggestion that he should start to lower the boats.

It was a similar story for Third Officer Pitman. When he first got up to the Boat Deck, he saw Bruce Ismay. Pitman did not immediately recognize Ismay, though it slowly dawned on him who he was.

Uncertain what to do, Pitman was soon chivvied up by Ismay who said quietly that 'there is no time to waste', a clear sign that the White Star Chairman was well aware how serious the problem was. Unsure what he should do, Pitman made his way to Captain Smith and told him that Ismay wished him to lower the boats. Smith replied: 'Go ahead, carry on'. Again, the Captain was responding to a question from his officer rather than taking proactive control of the situation.

Lawrence Beesley believed that Ismay transmitted the seriousness of the accident to many of the officers on deck. This begs a serious question, namely why Captain Smith did not proactively issue orders for the boats to be filled rather than rely on a company official to take the initiative in doing so. Smith also does not seem to have informed Lightoller of the parlous situation they were in which exacerbated an already dangerous state of affairs when the boats started to lower away soon after.

That lack of pro-activity was to have disastrous repercussions. Without clear instructions to follow, Lightoller decided to lower boats, with the exception of a few crew members to row, almost exclusively with women and children. While this might appear initially to be a gallant and chivalric gesture, it was one founded perhaps more on romanticism than common sense for many of the first boats to leave from the port side, where Lightoller was loading, were to go away half full.

At a later enquiry into the disaster, Lightoller would be directly asked why he had adopted this policy, which contributed significantly towards the loss of 500 lives that might have been saved. The Second Officer insisted that he had not filled the boats up more because he did not consider it safe to do so as the weight of a full boat might cause the ropes lowering her to break (evidently not correct as later on some would be lowered when nearly full). He repeatedly insisted later on emphasizing the difference between the lowering capacity and the floating capacity of a lifeboat. When pushed on the point as to why these first boats in particular were so empty, Lightoller came back with the damning reply 'because I did not know it was urgent then'.

This requires just a moment's reflection to see just how complete an indictment of the lack of leadership on the *Titanic* that night this comment is. Captain Smith and Thomas Andrews had been in early discussions when it appeared that the survival of the ship was highly unlikely. However, the Captain had not seen fit to let his Second

Officer, who was taking a leading role in loading the boats, in on the secret. It appears that the enormity of the crisis was overwhelming the great ship's captain.

Perhaps because of this lack of information, there was no panic in the loading of the boats until much later. The men, who were debarred from access on the port side, made no attempt to rush the boats; 'they could not have stood quieter if they had been in a church', Lightoller recalled. Seamen were deputed both to row the boats when they were afloat but also to help lower them, though there were too few of them and Lightoller would have trouble in manning them properly.

Boats with odd numbers were on the starboard side and were loaded mainly under the supervision of First Officer William Murdoch. The rule here was women and children only but men could go if there was room left for them. Those boats with even numbers were on the port side and were loaded under the watch of Lightoller. The rule here was women and children only. This was a policy followed with virtually no flexibility, an approach that sentenced dozens of men to death.

As Jack Thayer went out on deck, the noise of the steam escaping from the Titanic's funnels was still deafening. Jack and Milton Long tried to converse for a time but it was pointless so they went back inside into the crowded entrance hall where it was also much warmer. While they were there, they heard the stewards pass the word around that there were boats for them on the port side. Jack said goodbye to his mother and her maid at the top of the stairs on A Deck. The women then made their way out to the Boat Deck. Unknown to him, they were making for Boat Number 4, the launching of which would be a total fiasco.

Thayer father and son then made their way to the starboard side, probably thinking that this was where their boats would be lowered from. They could not understand what was happening; everybody was waiting for orders and no one was giving them. Few knew where their boat was as there had been no lifeboat drill. It was noisy but the deck was still well lit. People generally kept out of the way, letting the crew get on with their jobs, whatever they might be. Some second and third-class passengers soon started to arrive, making the crowd even larger.

The Collyers stood together waiting for a boat. Charlotte did not recognize anyone else around her and could not see anyone from first-class. Suddenly she saw a stoker come up from down below, his fingers badly cut, so much so that she thought they had been amputated. The sight suddenly sent a sensation of fear coursing through her. She noticed that First Officer Murdoch put guards by the gangways to stop anyone else coming up from down below.

Boat 4 was supposed to be the first boat lowered away, armed with orders to go around to the gangway. The Bosun's Mate was sent with a party of men to go and open the lower deck gangway door but they were never seen again, probably trapped in the maze of corridors as the invading sea rushed in. However, thanks to an aberration on Lightoller's part, this boat would not reach the water for over an hour.

The problem was that Lightoller ordered it lowered to A Deck. There were hawsers there that he thought he could tie the boat up against the side of the ship with. However, he forgot that this area was enclosed. He sent a steward down to open the windows but then decided that he might as well lower them from the Boat Deck after all. He had though in the meantime sent passengers like Mrs Emily Ryerson down to A Deck along with other women and children. Here they waited for further instructions, unaware for the moment that Lightoller had changed his mind. This was not a good time to be making things up as you went along.

The first steps had been taken to lowering the boat. Another harrowing suggestion of the serious situation the ship was in was about to appear. Captain Smith now decided that the ship should start to launch distress rockets. The task was delegated initially to Fourth Officer Boxhall. He pulled the rockets out of their storage cupboard and prepared one to fire. It shot up into the air, bursting at several hundred feet, exploding in a shower of white stars. There was a thud like a mortar shell. From the decks of the *Titanic*, necks craned upwards, those watching all of a sudden terribly aware of the danger they were in.

Fifth Officer Harold Lowe had been standing by Boat 3 when the first distress rocket flared up. It lit up the whole deck and there was a loud explosion which he found 'deafening'. It illuminated the nearby figure of Bruce Ismay, whose face must have been a picture of disbelief and shock. Lowe noticed that the Boat Deck was not crowded; just a 'little knot of people' gathered around the door of the gymnasium. There was still no sign of panic, yet the firing of the first rocket ratcheted up the tension by another notch.

The man-made stars bursting in the sky above the still ship woke people up to the emerging crisis. Everyone on the deck looked up in alarmed fascination as the rocket shot up into the ebony night and then erupted above them. As others started to follow, those aboard the *Titanic* now knew without a doubt that their ship, the 'practically unsinkable' vessel that was the biggest moving object ever built by man, was in distress.

As Beesley stood on the deck, two ladies approached a nearby officer and asked him if they could go onto the Boat Deck. He told them that they could not but should instead go to their own boats, pointing them elsewhere. They were second-class passengers and Beesley took the officer's actions as a sign that a form of class discrimination was being applied to filling the boats, though of course there is some logic in what the officer was saying as there were boats in the second-class part of the Boat Deck. However, when the policy was examined more closely it did not make sense at all; there were boats in first and second-class areas but none in third so where were third-class passengers supposed to go?

At this very moment, a rumour went around the starboard deck where Beesley was standing. It was to the effect that all male passengers were being lowered from the port side. Nothing, it transpired, could be further from the truth as Lightoller, who was in charge on that side, was lowering women and children only. But most of the men did make their way to the port side, leaving the starboard Boat Deck area virtually deserted. It was a sequence of events that, as Beesley later realized, led to his own personal salvation.

As he stood there (Beesley reckoned that the time was about 12.40 a.m.), a cellist from the ship's orchestra came round the corner, rushing down the deck and banging his cello on the planking as he did so. Beesley then looked over the side and saw that several boats were in the water. Officer Murdoch also leaned over and shouted to the boats to go around to the gangway door and wait to take off more passengers there. Murdoch then turned and walked back to the port side.

Boxhall started to fire these rockets off at roughly five minute intervals. It is debatable if this was in line with international distress regulations, which prescribed that rockets were to be fired off at short intervals – was five minutes a 'short interval' or not? But there was now a ray of hope for those on the ship. A light had been spotted just off the *Titanic*'s sagging bow. She was close enough for Captain Smith to tell Boxhall to try and contact her with a Morse lamp (a device that flashed out messages in Morse Code by sending light signals to match the 'dots' and 'dashes' of the code). This in itself suggested that she appeared to be quite close for it was unlikely that a Morse Lamp would be seen more than 10 miles away.

Boxhall was not sure of the colour of this other ship's lights at first but looked at her more closely through his binoculars. He first saw her two masthead lights, then her red side light. The distance that a red light was required to be visible for was 2 miles, again an indicator of how close the other ship was; Boxhall, who recalled that she had 'beautiful lights', estimated she was about 5 miles off, making allowances for the clearness of the night. He was also convinced that the ship he could see was moving. He had seen her green (starboard) sidelight at one stage but for most of the time could see her red (port) light. Captain Lord later told how his ship, somewhere to the north, slowly swung round after midnight because of the current 'and showed him [the ship nearby] our red light'. This too might be regarded as significant.

Boxhall's evidence about the ship he was watching moving towards them was one of Captain Lord's strongest arguments against the mystery ship being the *Californian*. Just about the only thing all witnesses from the *Californian* agree on is that the ship was motionless all night, apart from a very slow drift. If a ship was seen to be moving therefore, the argument ran, it could not be the *Californian* that the *Titanic*'s people could see.

The only problem with this apparently flawless argument is that Boxhall's evidence was contradicted by a number of other witnesses. Others who saw the light give very different accounts. Second Office Lightoller thought she was 'perfectly stationary', Pitman said that the light he saw had 'no motion in it, no movement'. Lowe saw the lights at two intervals an hour apart and they seemed to be in the same place while Fleet said: 'It never moved.' Steward Alfred Crawford also thought that they did not move. However, Quartermaster Hichens took the opposite view, telling the British Inquiry that 'the light was moving, gradually disappearing'. William Lucas saw the light and thought that it got further away every time they looked at it.

The eye-witness evidence of a stationary ship accords exactly with the situation aboard the *Californian* that night. Crawford in particular noted that the ship he could see was not at anchor – how could she be in the middle of the ocean – but was one that was moving irregularly because of the wind and current. That too was exactly what was happening to the *Californian*. But against that, the evidence of Boxhall, Lucas and Hichens suggests that the opposite was the case. The enigma of the so-called '*Californian* incident' that would later unfold is dogged by such contradictory evidence meaning that analysts can make pretty much what they want of it, ignoring some evidence and using other items to support their case as they wish.

Another contradictory witness now makes his appearance. At around 12.30 a.m., *Californian* time, Ernest Gill of that ship said he went out on deck for a cigarette. By this time, he could not see the ship he had spotted earlier. About ten minutes later he saw a rocket, which he thought was a shooting star. However when he saw another flash in the sky he realized what it was and was certain that it was a signal from a ship in distress. But he did nothing and, assuming the officers on the bridge would see it, he went back to bed. He was awoken at 6.30 a.m. next morning by the Chief Engineer of the *Californian* who told everyone to get up and prepare to render assistance as the *Titanic* had gone down.

Back on the *Titanic*, news had by now started to reach the passengers that a ship was on its way according to the wireless operators. This buoyed their spirits. Gracie pointed out to some of his fellow voyagers a white light on a ship 'which I took to be about 5 miles off and which I felt sure was coming to our rescue'. J.J. Astor asked Gracie to point it out, which he did. However, the light would prove to be a devastating disappointment; 'instead of growing brighter the light grew dim and less and less distinct and passed away altogether'.

When the order to lower away had been given, Gracie had escorted his charges up to the Boat Deck from A Deck. He saw Sixth Officer J.P. Moody barring the progress of all men passengers to the boats. He also saw a baker bringing out bread onto the deck to be loaded into the lifeboats, one of Joughin's entourage. One of Gracie's *coterie*, Miss Evans, told the Colonel that a fortune teller had told her to 'Beware of water' and that 'she now knew she would be drowned'.

Gracie then went to look for two acquaintances, Mrs Helen Candee and Mr Edward Kent. On the way he met Frank Wright, the squash professional onboard and remarked that they might have to postpone their game arranged for the morning after. Wright smiled hiding the truth; he knew that the squash court was already underwater.

Gracie returned to his stateroom to find it locked (he was looking for blankets). Steward Cullen told him that this was to prevent looting. They then went to get blankets together from the stewards' quarters. Gracie then went forward along A Deck still looking for his friends. In the smoking room, he found Archie Butt, military aide to President Taft, Clarence Moore and Francis Millet, the well-known artist (plus one unidentified individual) playing cards. No one else was there but they were playing as if they did not have a care in the world. Gracie never saw any of them again although a lady would tell him that she had seen Butt on the bridge just minutes before the last lifeboat rowed away (Gracie thinks it more likely that he stayed where he was; most of the card players bodies were ever found though Millet's was).

Gracie then returned to the port side, hovering between the Boat Deck and A Deck. He rejoined 'Clinch' Smith who told him that Mrs Candee was already off in a boat. He was on the Boat Deck when he heard the first rocket and then witnessed the *Titanic* Morsing for help. He saw no response from the ship in the distance and now feared for the first time that the *Titanic* might sink before all the lifeboats could be launched.

Boat 7 on the starboard side was probably the first one to be launched. Lookout Archie Jewell was in the boat (an odd statistic; there were six lookouts aboard *Titanic* and all of them survived). First Officer Murdoch had ordered women and children to the boats and then ordered Number 7 lowered away. The boat was to stand by the gangway. She remained the nearest to the *Titanic* for a time, even after other boats were lowered.

Mrs Helen Bishop, a first-class passenger, was also on the boat. She had been on deck and had seen the Captain tell Astor something in an undertone. Astor came over to Mrs Bishop, in a group of six women, and told them they should put their lifebelts on (they had left these down below). They all went to put them on and when they returned found very few people on deck. Mrs Bishop was pushed into the boat with her husband, Dickinson Bishop, and it was lowered with twenty-eight people aboard. Five people were transferred on to the boat from another one at a later stage but then she was rowed away to avoid the suction expected when the great ship went down.

French aviator Pierre Maréchal also got in. There was no rush at the boats, everything was calm and orderly. He heard no order of 'women and children first' or 'women and children only'. James McGough, another first-class passenger, also got in. He had also gone down to get his lifejacket and when he returned he saw the boats were being loaded. He said he *did* recall an order of 'women and children first'. There was some hesitation before anyone got into the boats. McGough insisted he was pushed in the boat by one of the officers (though of course such claims might be treated with cynicism; it was not 'heroic' for a first-class man to survive this disaster).

There was a significant sense of 'survivor guilt' among the men who survived the wreck. This was compounded by the veneer of heroism that contemporary society attached to those who went down on the ship. Men, especially, first-class men, were supposed to go down with the *Titanic* after giving up their places for women and children aboard. It was therefore difficult to explain how over fifty first-class men survived.

McGough was a perfect example of the dichotomy. He said that he was forced into Boat 7 so that he could row, implying there were not enough men in it. This does not make sense. There were fifteen men in this boat out of a total of twenty-eight people (he says there were forty). McGough's account hints at several pieces of what would now be called 'spin'. As well as his unconvincing reasons for his presence in the boat, his over-estimation of the number of people aboard in total was typical of virtually every account that appeared that discussed the subject of how many people were on each boat.

Quartermaster Alfred Olliver fumbled for the plug between the feet of the people in Boat 7 as it was lowered. When it hit the water, the sea started to rush in and Olliver had to scramble around to put the plug in properly. But at last she was safely down. Onboard her, those who had been lowered away looked up the huge sides of the ship, like a cliff towering above them in the darkness, not quite believing the situation that they were in.

As Lightoller passed along to Number 6 boat, he was conscious of the band playing *'jazz'* in the background. He was not a fan of such music but it gave a reassuring veneer of normality at a time like this. It would be lowered away just before 1.00 a.m. Capable of carrying sixty-five people, there were about twenty-eight aboard, a fitting precedent for what was to follow under Lightoller's watch. It would under the command of Quartermaster Hichens, the same man who had been at the helm when the berg had struck and had tried desperately to avoid it.

First-class passenger 'Madame de Villiers' appeared, dressed in a nightgown and slippers; Margaret Brown noticed she had no stockings on but that she had a long woollen motoring overcoat over her. Realizing the seriousness of the situation where presumably she had not done so before, she was going to go back to her cabin to pick up her valuables when Mrs Brown talked her out of it. After some hesitation, 'Madame de Villiers' got into the lifeboat.

'Madame de Villiers' however did not exist. She was in fact Berthe Antonine Mayné, a Belgian cabaret singer. Her life story might come as a surprise to those who think this was a puritanical, prudish era. She was described in one contemporary publication as 'being well known in Brussels in circles of pleasure, and was often seen in the company of people who like to wine and dine and enjoy life' – the last phrase in particular might be a hint at all kinds of vices. During the winter of 1911, she had met a young Canadian hockey player, Quigg Baxter, while performing. The two soon became lovers. 'Madame de Villiers' had been installed in first-class cabin C90. Now she bade farewell to Baxter on the deck of the *Titanic*. A tragic *denouement* to this passionate affair was fast approaching.

Mrs Brown in the meantime started to walk away to see what was happening elsewhere. However, she had barely moved when someone caught her by the arm insisting that she too got in a boat. She was dropped 4 feet into the lifeboat. As the boat was lowered it was nearly swamped by a stream of water coming through a porthole from D Deck. Margaret Brown grabbed an oar and pushed the boat away from the side of the deck. When they reached the water, as flat as a millpond, she looked up and saw Captain Smith looking down at them. He told them to pull for the light in the distance.

Mrs Helen Candee, also in Boat 6 (the lady that Gracie had been looking in vain for), handed an ivory miniature of her mother to Mr Edward Kent (it was later recovered from his body). He was reluctant to take it, perhaps seeing it as a bad omen or having a premonition that he would not survive. When the boat was half lowered, it was noticed that there was only one man in it. Lightoller looked for a volunteer and Major Peuchen climbed out along a spar and down a rope into it, drawing on skills he had gained as an experienced yachtsman. As the boat began to be lowered, Peuchen was conscious of rockets being fired off and exploding over the ship.

The shortage of men in Boat 6 had arisen because of some confusion in loading it. Seaman Samuel Hemming had been in the boat helping to load it and Lightoller had assumed he would go with it. However, Hemming had stepped out of the boat at the last minute, thinking that he was more useful on deck. Unaware of the fact,

Lightoller had lowered the boat with only one man aboard, hence the need for Peuchen's acrobatic performance. Peuchen anyway later wondered why boats were not being lowered with more people in them. However, he later had to live down the fact that he was a man who had survived the *Titanic* – a quite nonsensical attitude given the fact that he had been ordered into a half-empty lifeboat with hardly any men in it to row it.

Peuchen commented later on the perfect discipline on the ship. He also noticed 'about 100' stokers on deck before the boat was launched; an officer came along and drove them all off the boat deck as if they had no right to be there. However, Mrs Candee also noticed this but saw it rather differently, praising the men for the way in which they obeyed the order when they could have overrun the boat if they had wished. She also noted the brave behaviour of her steward; when she advised him to save himself too, he replied that there was 'plenty of time for that' – he would not survive.

When Mrs Candee entered the boat, she slipped on the oars and broke her ankle. The lowering of the boat proved difficult and jerky; and she was in agony but also terrified that the boat at one stage would be swamped. On getting onto the boat, Peuchen had fumbled in the dark for the plug. He could not find it. Hichens shouted: 'Hurry up, this boat is going to founder!' Peuchen thought he meant the lifeboat but he did not; he meant the *Titanic*. Lookout Frederick Fleet and Peuchen were then responsible for the rowing.

They later discovered an 'Italian' 'stowaway' in the boat; he had a broken wrist and was no help in the rowing. However, this disdainful slur with its racist connotations that Peuchen directed implicitly at him was unwarranted on two counts. It seems likely that he was an injured boy ordered in by the Captain, and Mrs Candee also did not think that he was an Italian.

Frederick Fleet could see a white light. The boat's untrained crew headed for it, shining brightly over on their port bow. But it seemed to be pulling away from them all the time. It is interesting that Fleet, who had not been able to see a light from the crow's nest where he had been until 12.23 a.m. could now see one when he was almost at sea level half an hour later.

Major Peuchen could also see something but believed it to be a reflection, 'an imaginary light' as he called it rather than a genuine sign of hope. Mrs Lucian Smith, also in Boat 6, believed it to be a star. Peuchen thought that it was to the north of *Titanic*, a compass bearing he worked out from the direction of the Northern Lights (though not everyone agreed; Third Officer Pitman thought it was to the west). Lightoller, when lowering the boat, had told Hichens, who was in charge of it, to 'pull toward that light'. Hichens, who thought he was looking at a trawler, proceeded to do so.

Peuchen's comments on the light are interesting, as they suggest just how many different versions of it many witnesses saw that night. Peuchen did not think that 'from my knowledge of yachting that it was a boat light. The northern lights were very strong that night. It might have been some reflection on ice. I was not satisfied it was the light of a steam by any means.' Contrast this view of a yachtsman and a man who was on his fortieth trans-Atlantic crossing, with that of an experienced sailor like Fourth Officer Boxhall who believed that he *was* looking at a steamer with green and red lights showing and you have a neat example of the dichotomy of evidence concerning any so-called 'mystery ship'.

There were though a large number of witnesses who saw the light, though they did not agree on what kind of ship it was or indeed if it was a ship at all. Quartermaster Alfred Olliver, in Boat 5, could not be sure whether the light he could see belonged to a ship or a star. But Able Seaman George Moore's boat, Number 3, which would be launched soon after, rowed for a bright light just 2–3 miles away on the starboard bow. He too thought it was a trawler.

With the loading of the boats underway, Lightoller would get into a rhythm. Each boat was lowered until its gunwales were level with the Boat Deck. He would then stand with one foot on the gunwales, the other on the deck, take women and children by the arm and virtually lift them over the gap. Two crew men were deputed to accompany each boat but it was not long before he was short of them. With the ship now starting to dip lower, it was important that he developed an efficient loading process.

Third Officer Pitman was loading up Boat 5. There was a big crowd around the boat. He asked for more women but there were none to be seen so he let a 'few' men in – this does not ring true, as statistics prepared later suggest that there were as many men as women in the boat. The embarrassment felt by male survivors who did not live up to the heroic idealistic picture that was later developed was evidenced by Pitman's subsequent statements to the US Inquiry. Here he stated that there were half a dozen men in the boat – other evidence suggests that there were in fact at least ten. Murdoch told Pitman he was in charge and to row around to the gangway and take more passengers off. By the time the boat was lowered away, Trimmer Hemming had not managed to provide her with a light.

Steward Etches also perpetuated the myth of men giving up their places for women. He later said that Boat 5 took in thirty-six ladies. However, there were only forty people in the boat, of whom fifteen or more were men. Bruce Ismay was on the scene. He called out asking if there were any more women to be loaded. One appeared, a stewardess, who was loaded onto the boat. She would not initially get in because 'I am only a stewardess'. Bruce Ismay said: 'No matter, you are a woman, take your place.'

As the boat was being lowered, a German-American physician, Doctor Frauenthal and his brother, jumped in. This created some controversy. Mrs Annie Stengel, a first-class passenger, was on the boat. She stated that her husband, Charles, drew back from the boat but that four men proceeded to jump in as it was being lowered; these presumably included Frauenthal and his brother, who was also there. Frauenthal she thought weighed about 250 pounds and was wearing two life preservers. He wanted to be with his wife, who was also in the boat. This was perhaps understandable as they had only been married for two weeks. However, on the way in he struck Mrs Stengel forcefully, breaking several of her ribs.

First-class passenger Norman Chambers also got in, he said because his wife would have got out if he did not. But all this nonsense about men getting into the boats was rather fatuous. There was still room for twenty-five passengers in the boat when it was lowered and there were no women around. Mrs Stengel also protested too much (though perhaps her cracked ribs provided some justification); her husband later got off in another boat. Another first-class passenger, George Harder, said that the lowering of the boat was jerky but they got down safely enough. There was trouble with getting the plug in and also cutting the boat free from the *Titanic*. He suggests there were hardly any men on the boat, which is simply not true.

While on the Boat Deck, Chambers could hardly hear himself think, the terrific noise of steam escaping making it virtually impossible to hear anybody in the vicinity. As his boat was being filled, he did hear an officer say 'that is enough before lowering. We can get more in after she is in the water'. His boat was then lowered. Damning the sailors responsible for looking after the boats with faint praise, Chambers later remarked harshly but truthfully: 'We were then lowered away in a manner which I would consider very satisfactory, taking into account the apparent absolute lack of training of the rank and file of the crew.' Mrs Anna Warren said that by the time she reached the Boat Deck there were not many people there. She also heard a deafening roar of escaping steam. Mr and Mrs Astor were close by but did not try and get in this boat but went back inside (perhaps J.J. Astor's best chance to survive had been missed). When it came to the time to lower the boat, both men and women moved towards it. Mr Warren was assisting women on the deck elsewhere and she did not see him again. The boat was only lowered she thought with great difficulty and Mrs Warren was worried that the boat would be swamped when it hit the sea.

Also onboard Number 5 was Paul Maugé, clerk in the Ritz kitchen. He had been billeted in third-class quarters. He awoke after the collision and went up to see what was going on. He went to wake up the chef and then returned through the second-class saloon. Here, he saw that the kitchen assistants were not allowed up onto the boat deck. When Maugé saw the boat being lowered, he jumped into it. He advised the chef to copy his example but he was too portly to do so. Once Maugé was in the boat he told the chef to jump once more but again he was unwilling to do so. As the boat was lowered, members of the crew still onboard the *Titanic* tried to pull Maugé out but were unable to do so. He saw no passengers being prevented from entering the Boat Deck but thought he was let past because he was not dressed like a member of the crew.

There was some debate about how many these boats would hold. First-class passenger George Harder, who had come aboard at Cherbourg, counted thirty-six people in the boat. He was aware that it was said that the boats would hold sixty people but he did not believe they could; even with this number in, she seemed full. It is not immediately obvious how then some boats were filled by the end of the night with twice as many people as this.

Fifth Officer Lowe had helped to load the boat and had almost come to blows with Bruce Ismay in the process. Ismay was desperate to get the boats off as quickly as possible. According to the officer, he was 'overanxious and he was getting a trifle excited'. Urged to move more quickly, the hot-headed Welshman turned on him and told him, 'If you will get the hell out of it I shall be able to do something. Do you want me to lower away quickly? You will have me drown the lot of them.' Ismay, publicly berated, sloped off to Boat 5. Seasoned older hands looked on in horror, sure that there would be a reckoning at a later stage.

Third Officer Pitman ordered the boat to pull far enough away to avoid suction when the *Titanic* went down. As they moved away, they realized that the ship was going down slowly by the head. The full horror of what was slowly happening to the great ship was more apparent from the sea than it was onboard. However, even then there were still those who thought that the ship would not sink. Pitman was convinced she would stay afloat. It would be another hour before he believed the ship was doomed.

This might be why these first boats were lowered with spaces for many others on them. It was a policy that inspired perhaps one of the most memorable quotes of that memorable night. Stoker Walter Hurst watched on disbelievingly and commented: 'If they are sending the boats away, they might as well put some people in them.'

It was a problem that Dr Washington Dodge noticed too. He watched on as the boats began to be lowered. He was not impressed by what he saw. Not a boat would pull away he noted that would not have taken between ten and twenty-five more people. He saw no women or children on decks and observed that, as soon as everyone in the immediate vicinity had been got aboard, the boats were lowered away. This made sense provided that all passengers had been brought to the Boat Deck so that they could take their places in the boats. This of course was not the case. If there was no one else to load and the boats were being lowered only half full, yet there were not enough places available for half those aboard, then huge numbers of passengers were being kept in some place other than the Boat Deck. Major Peuchen was insistent: 'Every woman on the port side was given an opportunity. In fact, we had not enough women to put into the boats. We were looking for them. I cannot understand why we did not take some men. The boats would have held more.' Here were several valid observations. Firstly, there were no more women to load but a number of women would be lost. Therefore, there were not proper arrangements in place for making sure that all the women were being brought up to the Boat Deck.

Also, Lightoller and Wilde on the port side should have been allowing more men into the boats. For men to give up their lives to let women off in the boats might be regarded as chivalrous. For them to give up their lives when boats were being lowered half empty might be regarded as pointless.

But even the officers seemed unsure how many a boat could safely hold. Lowe reckoned that the maximum lowering capacity of a sixty-five-person boat was fifty. This was twice as many as Lightoller, who reckoned that the lowering capacity was an incredible twenty-five people only. There were also problems emerging concerning the number of seamen available to row. A number had been sent to open gangway doors so that more people could get off when the boats were in the water. They never returned and were presumably lost. Now some boats were being lowered with hardly any seamen in them. A proper boat drill might have helped.

Stewardess Violet Jessop was now up on deck after staying down in her cabin in the 'glory hole', as the steward's quarters were known, for a while after the collision. She and her room-mate remained there for a time until a steward came to fetch them, hurrying them up as, he explained, the boat was sinking and they needed to get off. There was a bizarre exchange while they argued about what to wear including which hat was the most appropriate attire to wear in a lifeboat.

When she went outside, the coldness of the night air had caught Violet by surprise so she went below to pick up more clothes. Passing an open cabin, she saw an eiderdown, which she went in to get. She threw it around her shoulders. She noticed the empty rooms, still well lit, with jewels left lying on dressing-room tables and in one a pair of silver slippers thrown off carelessly by someone in their haste to get dressed and away.

On her way back to the Boat Deck, she had passed a group of four officers casually standing and chatting. They smiled and waved in recognition as she passed. She later said that the four men were Captain Smith, Ismay, Purser McElroy and Doctor O'Loughlin though as she supplied these names four decades after the event we cannot be sure that her memory was not mistaken.

On her way up, she also passed a young woman remonstrating with an officer who was refusing to allow her father to accompany her into a boat. He had explained that the decks must be cleared of women and children before any men would be allowed through. She had then met Jock Hume, the violinist of the band, who were getting ready to play at the time. He was a great friend of Violet and he explained to her that they were going to provide music to keep the passengers' spirits up.

Two pantry boys appeared carrying bread to load onto the lifeboats. Despite the signs of serious events unfolding, there was no panic on deck. It helped that people could see the ship's lights on the horizon;

these were frequently being pointed out. In fact, she noted that those on the ship cheered up as the light appeared to be coming closer. Nevertheless, someone suggested to the officer in charge of loading that the boats were being lowered with too few people on them and, when he decided to put more in, there was a surge as people pushed forward trying to get aboard one.

Amid all the signs of impending doom, one small loss of crew discipline struck home to Violet, the sight of a steward standing with cigarette in hand. It was unthinkable in normal circumstances that a member of the crew would do so amid all the passengers and it was a sign of the erosion of the supposedly unbreachable barriers between crew and passengers that forcibly brought home the nature of the situation they were all in. It is interesting that several of the passengers would later complain of crew smoking in their presence.

Passengers kept on coming up to Lightoller and asking them if the situation was serious. He kept on smiling back at them, saying that the loading of the boats was just a precaution. Yet the frequent trails from distress rockets being fired high into the night sky gave the lie to his reassurances. The cascade of stars that spangled forth when they exploded added a distinctly ominous tint to the atmosphere.

Lightoller too could see the light of a ship. He estimated that it was just a few miles away. He reasoned that the boats would soon be picked up. He carried on with his plan to open the gangway doors, ask the boats to stand off by them and pick up more passengers from his sinking ship. Although it suggests a plan of sorts, it was unnecessarily complex. The boats could be lowered with a full complement without buckling. Lightoller's plan added unnecessary time and complexity when time was short and simplicity highly desirable. It was a mistake, as his captain should have told him. But Captain Smith remained peripheral.

Steward Hart had arrived with his batch of third-class passengers from down below. He had about thirty women and children in tow. He took them to the side of Boat 8 and left them there. However, it was not immediately obvious that he had not been wasting his time for none of them got off in it. This was incredible; the boat had a capacity of sixty-five but only had about thirty people in it when it was lowered. Hart in the meantime had gone down below to pick up more third-class passengers and bring them back up to the Boat Deck.

The single male passengers billeted forward in the ship had been flooded out and forced towards the rear of the ship. They made their way along the corridor known as Scotland Road carrying their baggage with them. Many of them were foreigners without a word of English. Interpreter Müller had his work cut out helping them out. Despite that, there seemed to be no chaos or panic among them at this stage.

Boat 3 on the starboard side would be lowered at about 1.00 a.m. Able Seaman George Moore helped load the boat. Once more, there were not enough women on the Boat Deck to fill it with female passengers, so when there were no women left, the men were loaded. 'There were a few men passengers', Moore later said, not wishing to puncture any myths; however, this was a very misleading statement. There were about ten male passengers out of the thirty in the boat and, when members of the crew were taken into account (there were a large number of stokers in it) the men aboard comfortably outnumbered the women. Strangely, try as he might Lowe could not find any more passengers to put in the boat.

Elizabeth Shute was one of those who did get in. She felt that the boat had been lowered amid the greatest confusion. Orders were shouted by rough seamen, left, right and centre. As the boat was lowered the 70 feet or so to the icy Atlantic, the falls stuck and one side started to dip down faster than the other, threatening to throw all its occupants into the sea. With difficulty, the problem was addressed and at last Boat 3 reached the sea in safety, though to Miss Shute the open sea did not seem a very safe place to be.

Way down in the bowels of the ship, matters had taken a significant turn for the worse unknown to those on deck. At around 12.45 a.m. Boiler Room 5 was almost empty. However firemen Fred Barrett had stayed below with a few mates to operate the pumps in an effort to buy some more time. One of them, Second Engineer Jonathan Shepherd had fallen down a manhole and broken his leg. He had been taken to a pump room to try and make him comfortable.

While Barrett and Second Engineer Herbert Harvey valiantly continued their efforts, all of a sudden things took a dramatic twist. Without any warning, the bulkhead between Boiler Rooms 5 and 6 suddenly disintegrated. A torrent of water, cold and chilling, burst through. Barrett climbed as quickly as he could up the escape ladder. As he turned, he saw Harvey heroically rush towards Shepherd to try and get him out. He was too late. Shepherd was completely engulfed by the onrushing wave.

This was a terrible personal disaster but it was also another fatal blow for the ship. *Titanic* had taken another hit, another cavernous boiler room was flooded and the ship lurched further down at the head. The terrible mathematical certainty that the ship must sink as each successive compartment was filled and the vessel tipped lower in the water was starting to dawn on most of those onboard.

In contrast, it was hard to imagine a quieter night than the one being experienced by the *Californian*. Stopped in the ice, the ship had effectively closed down. Captain Lord had been down in the chart room, reading and enjoying a smoke. At about 12.35 a.m. *Californian* time, Lord had called up to the bridge through the speak tube in the chart room. He wanted to know if the ship he had seen earlier had moved any closer. Stone replied that there had been no change at all in her position.

It is important to note that, at this time at least, there was nothing to alert the suspicions of anyone aboard the *Californian*. The nearby ship had stopped and had not attempted to contact them, either by Morse lamp (not all ships had them) or rocket. She appeared to be doing exactly what Lord was doing, namely stopping for the ice until daybreak enabled her to find a way through. Lord decided to turn in for a few hours sleep. It had been a long and draining day. He told Stone to contact him if he needed anything and, still fully dressed, stretched out on the sofa in the chart room and began to doze off. He was soon in a deep sleep.

Second Officer Herbert Stone was now on his own. The apprentice, James Gibson, had gone off on an errand and Stone had the bridge to himself. He kept an eye on the ship to the south, staring at her with his binoculars from time to time. He paced slowly backwards and forwards across the bridge. It was about 12.45 a.m., ship's time, when he thought he saw a flash in the sky. He thought that it was a shooting star, of which he had seen a number that night. Now though his attention was firmly fixed on the nearby ship.

As he watched, there was another flash followed by several more at intervals. He could not though make out what they were. He was unsure whether they were signals of some sort, recognition devices used by ships at sea, or something of more sinister import. However, he was puzzled by them, more than anything else by their low altitude and the fact that they did not appear to be coming from the nearby ship. He was uncertain what to do so for the time being he took the most unsatisfactory option possible; he did nothing.

The rockets were undoubtedly unusual but he could not believe there was anything to worry about. And so as, somewhere not too far off, the boats of the doomed leviathan were lowered into the water, those on watch on the *Californian* went about their business as if this was just another quiet night in the North Atlantic.

5

The Looming Crisis

01.01–01.30, 15 April 1912

On the *Titanic*, the atmosphere was still fairly calm, though there was an increasing sense of anxiety developing. Boats had started to be lowered and rockets had been fired, both signs that those in command of the ship were concerned that the ship was in danger. However, *Titanic* was so big, so substantial, so solid. It was still inconceivable to many that she might sink.

To the south, the *Carpathia* was now hurrying with all the speed she could muster to the rescue. It was clear to those commanding her that the situation onboard the *Titanic* was parlous. They received a message from the *Titanic* at around 1.00 a.m. *Carpathia* time, stating laconically 'engine room nearly full' – presumably this was not long after Leading Stoker Fred Barrett had been flooded out when the bulkhead collapsed down below. There was no time to lose and Captain Rostron anxiously watched as the minutes ticked past in this race against time.

The passengers gathered around the lifeboats on *Titanic*'s Boat Deck. There was an emphasis on women and children being lowered away first but some women refused to go, wives who would not be parted from husbands or children from parents. Charlotte Collyer was one of them. She saw Harold Lowe loading the boats; despite his youth, he had a presence about him which imposed itself on others who felt compelled to obey his instructions. One passenger in particular seemed to her to be interfering too readily in the boat-loading. She had seen Lowe ordering him away peremptorily. Only later did she think that the busybody passenger was J. Bruce

Ismay. However, at some stage he moved off to load other boats and Charlotte Collyer lost sight of him.

Colonel Gracie had initially been kept back from the boats but the policy had now changed and he was not prevented from approaching them. Wanting to be helpful, he started to play a role in loading them, there being in his opinion no time to lose. He was now on A Deck, where boats were being loaded having been lowered from the Boat Deck. Lightoller was standing, one foot in the lifeboat, the other on the rail of the deck, his stentorian voice, with its lilting accent, giving firm instructions to those getting on the boats. Women, children and babies were passed through the open window to him.

A staircase led from the Boat Deck directly down to C Deck and Lightoller went down it every so often to gauge the water's progress. He watched with horrified fascination as step by step the water started to climb the stairs, the electric lights that it devoured burning on for a few eerie seconds before they at last went out forever; Lightoller recalled that this weird sight created a 'ghastly transparency'. The deck lights were still on though which meant that the dynamos were still doing their work. One woman waved a cane with an electric light in it, almost blinding Lightoller as he worked. This was Mrs J. Stuart White and, however inconvenient her cane might have been at the time, it would do good service later on (or so she claimed).

Mrs White gives the impression of being someone who would now be euphemistically described as 'high maintenance'. She was in many ways the epitome of the first-class passenger, spoilt and pampered. She comes across as being something of a metaphorical bulldog and, without wishing to be disrespectful, her photographs suggest an uncanny physical resemblance to one too. She was convinced that none of the men were particularly heroic that night for the simple reason that none of them thought the ship would sink so they were quite safe staying where they were. As she prepared to leave the ship, she heard comments from them suggesting that they would all need passes to get back onboard in the near future.

She was not impressed at the quality of the crew onboard the lifeboat either. She was shocked to hear them asked, before they got in, whether or not they could row. She had a point, as it transpired that very few of them could and some of the women had to help out. It was a shame, Mrs White grumbled, that the crew were in the boat at the expense of some of the men passengers, 'athletes and men of sense', as she called them; she was presumably referring to the first-class element.

As the seriousness of the ship's position was now becoming more obvious, Lightoller now ordered the boats filled to the maximum capacity he dared. It is certainly true that later boats would have more people on them than those loaded at the beginning but it is equally true that they still had space in them. Lightoller was struck by the calmness of those entrapped in the looming crisis. There was a young honeymoon couple on deck, walking calmly up and down. The new husband asked Lightoller if there were anything he could do to help.

While he was loading the boats, Chief Officer Wilde asked Lightoller if he knew where the firearms were. They were not needed yet and were merely being sought as a precaution. Murdoch did not know where they were so Lightoller went, accompanied by him, the Chief Officer and Captain Smith to the place where the firearms were stored. As they left, the Chief Officer handed a pistol to Lightoller. Not thinking he would need it, he put it carelessly in his pocket along with a few cartridges.

As he returned to his post, Lightoller saw Mr and Mrs Straus standing by the deck house. He asked Mrs Straus if he could take her along to the boats but she replied in the negative. Mr Straus tried to persuade her but she was not having any of it. Neither was another unnamed young woman who was sitting on deck with her husband. Lightoller asked her to if she wished to be escorted to a boat. Her reply was immediate: 'Not on your life, we started together, and if need be, we will finish together.'

Lightoller continued to look at the nearby ship as his own sank lower. He could not understand why she did not respond to the *Titanic's* frequent requests for help. He had been reassuring passengers all the time he had been lowering the boats with her presence but it was increasingly obvious that she was not going to come to the rescue. The frustration and desperation that must have been felt is unimaginable.

Jack Thayer and his father now decided that they ought to make sure that Mrs Thayer had safely got into a boat. Down on B Deck, the lounge was full of people and they had to push their way out onto the open deck through a crowd. The crush was so great that Jack and Milton Long were separated from Thayer Senior. Jack would never see his father again. At the time, he assumed that both his mother and father would make their way safely onto a lifeboat and he made his way to the starboard side with Milton Long to see whether there was any chance of getting off there.

By now, Jack noticed that the bows of the great ship were underwater. He said later that he could still see the boats 500 or 600 feet away though as only one of them had a light and it was such a dark night this was doubtful unless he could see them in the reflected glare of the rockets that were still shooting up every five minutes or so. But he insisted that they were 'plainly visible' so perhaps the starlight was indeed bright enough to illuminate the scene.

The lights were still burning on the great ship and the exhaust steam was still roaring. The band continued to play, though they had life preservers on by now. Thayer noticed a man come through the door carrying a bottle of Gordon's Gin which he had been liberally helping himself to. He told himself that he would, for certain, not be one of those lucky enough to survive the night but he was wrong.

The irony was that Jack Thayer and his father did not know that his mother, waiting to get in Boat 4, was still on the *Titanic*. Lightoller kept changing his mind about where the boat should be lowered from. He had first of all decided that it should be filled from A Deck and then changed his mind to the Boat Deck after being reminded that A Deck was enclosed. He now changed his mind again; she would be filled from A Deck after all from the opened windows.

Steward George Dodd told the passengers waiting to go back to A Deck. Mrs Thayer was getting annoyed at this to-ing and fro-ing, with every justification. This was not just inconvenient, it was also clear that there was real danger on the ship and time was of the essence. Another person waiting to get on Boat 4, Mrs Martha Stephenson said that when they came up the stairs onto the Boat Deck they saw Captain Smith, looking very worried. The ship was listing heavily to port. She saw the rockets going up, which alarmed her. It suggested that any wireless messages that had been sent were not having any effect and that the situation was growing serious.

However, the sense of urgency had not yet fully transmitted itself to the people responsible for filling the boats. Boat 8 was about to be filled. It had a capacity of sixty-five people; survivors' accounts suggest that between twenty-eight and thirty-five would actually get in it, including Mrs J. Stuart White. Able Seaman Thomas Jones was one of those aboard. As he got in the boat, Captain Smith was on hand, asking him if the plug was in the boat; he replied in the affirmative. He then asked for any more ladies but there were none.

The Captain and a steward then helped drop the boat gently down
the side of the ship. Captain Smith had also instructed Steward Alfred
Crawford to get in, pull for the light and land the boat there and then
come back for more passengers.

The Captain of the *Titanic* clearly thought that the mystery ship
was very close if this was his expectation. Crawford believed he
could see two lights, one on the foremast, one on the main of this
mysterious vessel. 'Everybody saw them' was his assessment but they
could make no headway towards reaching them. Crawford reckoned
it was at most 10 miles away and was sure that it was a steamer as a
sailing ship would not have two lights. As he pulled away from the
Titanic, he saw that she was making water fast at the bows.

Mrs Straus had at one stage started to get into Boat 8, along with
her maid. However, when she had one foot on the gunwale she
stepped out again and stood by her husband. She said defiantly: 'We
have been living together for many years, and where you go, I go.' The
Strauses then sat themselves down in deck chairs on the enclosed A
Deck, waiting for their fate. Someone suggested to Mr Straus that no
one would object if an old man got in a boat but he was not having
any of it. He would not seek to gain an advantage over other men.
The irony of course is that if he had gone to the other side of the ship,
he would have had no problem in getting in a lifeboat with a clear
conscience.

Fourth Officer Boxhall had been frantically trying to contact
the nearby ship with a Morse lamp and frustratingly was getting
nowhere. Worse than this, as the night wore on she turned around
and presented her stern light as if she was preparing to move away.
He could not make out what she was but was convinced that she was
not a fishing boat. Rockets still shot up at regular intervals. By now,
Boxhall had been joined by Quartermaster Rowe. However, the other
ship seemed to be taking not a blind bit of notice of them.

In the meantime, Second Officer Stone on the *Californian* was
increasingly confused. By 1.15 a.m. *Californian* time he had seen five
rockets shoot up into the air. It is now that we enter the murkiest,
muddiest, most indecipherable part of the story of the so-called
Californian incident.

Stone had seen five rockets, all white. He said in a signed statement
later that he informed Lord of the fact: 'I, at once, whistled down the
speaking tube and you came from your chartroom into your own
room and answered.' The phrasing would imply that he immediately

told Lord of the rockets (Gibson said that Stone had told him that he had reported to Lord after he had seen the second rocket) but exactly how many he had seen when he reported to Lord is somewhat ambiguous in Stone's statement.

Lord seemed to confirm that some time had elapsed before the rockets were reported to him. In his own later affidavit, he confirmed that he was informed of the situation by Stone 'at about 1.15 a.m.'. However, this is directly contradicted by the evidence given by Apprentice James Gibson in a statement given immediately after the disaster and before any formal Inquiries had begun on 18 April.

Gibson's recollection was that he had been below decks and had returned to the bridge at about 12.55 a.m. Stone had told him that the other ship had fired five rockets and he had already reported the fact to Lord after he had spotted the second one. This would have put the time closer to 12.45 a.m. than 1.15 a.m. *Californian* time. Stone however also thought it was about 1.15 a.m. Two to one evidence; that is about the best odds one could get on anything reported from the *Californian* that night.

Informed of the rockets, Gibson had first of all tried to contact the ship with the Morse light but got no response. He then picked up his binoculars and trained them on the ship. He was actually looking through these when 'I observed a white flash apparently on her deck, followed by a faint streak towards the sky which then burst into white stars. Nothing then happened until the other ship was about two points on the starboard bow when she fired another rocket.' Stone thought that the rockets were appearing very low down, and may well have come from a point beyond and behind the ship he was watching. Gibson however clearly thought that the rockets were coming from the ship he could see. The fact that Gibson was actually watching through binoculars when the rockets were fired makes his account the more difficult to refute.

No one on the *Titanic* saw any rockets fired from any other ship that night, at least not until several hours later when the *Carpathia* was steaming towards the lifeboats. Therefore, it is almost certain that the only ship firing rockets in the area that night was the *Titanic*. If Gibson was right and the ship he was watching was also the ship firing rockets (and the ones he saw were white as were those fired by Fourth Officer Boxhall), then the ship he could see must have been the *Titanic*.

Lord's recollection of the conversation he had with Stone earlier (which of course Gibson did not hear as he was not on the bridge at the time) contradicted Stone in several crucial details. Stone reported 'seeing lights in the sky in the direction of the other steamer which appeared to me to be white rockets'. Lord however recollected that Stone had reported to him that the other steamer 'had fired a white rocket' in the singular. Stone's recollection was that he reported to Lord after seeing the fifth rocket. Gibson's account of what happened is more ambiguous and suggests that Stone may have reported the rockets after seeing the second one (Gibson was not there at the time so was quoting second-hand).

There are two important differences to emphasize here. Firstly Stone said that the rockets came from the direction of the other ship. Lord recollected that he had told him that the signals came from the other ship itself, not just from her general direction, a point of view that corroborates Gibson's opinion that the rockets came from the nearby ship (though of course Lord had not seen any rockets himself and might merely have misheard Stone or drawn the wrong conclusion). Secondly, Stone said he reported rockets in the plural, Lord only remembered hearing of one in the singular.

Reading Stone's version it is easy to interpret the situation as being that the ship he could see and the rockets were not directly connected; that is indeed consistent with his other evidence when he thought that the rockets came 'from a good distance beyond her'. However, Lord believed that the rockets were coming from the ship itself as did Gibson.

Secondly, it is perhaps easy enough to dismiss one isolated rocket as nothing too much to worry about. Company recognition signals were sometimes used back then. However, Stone had seen more than one when he reported to Lord. To anyone attuned to imminent danger (which Lord, as his earlier precautions attested, was) then being aware of this many rockets might have suggested that a serious situation was unfolding not far away from him. But amazingly, if Stone did report the rockets after seeing just two of them, he then saw three more rockets before Gibson came back and did not report further to Lord until much, much later.

There was also another man who claimed to have seen the rockets. This was 'donkeyman' Ernest Gill (a donkeyman was the quaint name for an engineer from the engine room). He was back on deck he said, having another cigarette, at about 12.30 a.m. He was standing there for about ten minutes when he saw a white rocket, though he too thought at first that it was a shooting star. Just short of ten minutes later, he saw another flash and thought to himself that 'that must be a vessel in distress'.

This appears to be fairly decisive evidence but there are several flaws with it. It has been suggested by some that Gill is an unreliable witness, partly on the grounds that he confessed to some of his shipmates that he expected to make money from his story (though this in itself does not mean that it is false). However, it was a freezing cold night and he must have been finding it very difficult to sleep if he chose to spend this length of time in the open.

Most difficult to explain away is what he did *not* see. He said that now there was no ship in sight, he could just see the rockets about 10 miles away. But both Stone and Gibson quite clearly saw both a ship and the rockets at around the same time.

There was also the problem of what Gill did *not* do. He did not report the rockets to anyone else at the time. He said, 'It was not my business to notify the bridge or the lookout but they could not have helped but see them. I turned in immediately after, supposing the ship would pay attention to the rockets.' At best this shows a seriously cavalier attitude and an astonishing lack of any sense of responsibility. It is easy to see why those who felt that Captain Lord was unfairly singled out as the villain of the piece did their best to discredit Gill as a witness, suggesting that he merely developed the story after the event in an attempt to make some money out of the disaster.

Neither did it help Gill's case when he was inconsistent in the accounts he gave at different times in his later evidence. In his original affidavit Gill described how he had seen 'a big vessel going along at full speed' at around midnight. By the time that he got to London he was much less confident, merely saying that 'I did not stand to look at the ship but I supposed she would be moving'.

He would also say to the British Inquiry that he could not be sure that what he had seen was a company recognition signal or a rocket. However, when asked if he regarded the rocket as being of any significance he said: 'No, not any importance. It was a signal... ' This is very different from being convinced that he was watching a ship in distress. He could not even be sure what direction the ship he was watching was travelling.

Captain Lord would later be publicly castigated for his inaction and would vigorously deny that he had been close enough to the *Titanic* to make any difference to the situation. He would argue that the ship that could be seen close to his was emphatically not the *Titanic*. A brutal war of accusation and counter-accusation would break out. People would take sides in a battle between the so-called 'pro-Lordites' and the 'anti-Lordites'. The debate continues to this day, fought out with huge passion and partisanship by supporters and opponents of Captain Lord alike.

The weapons used by the participants include bewildering (and ultimately currently unprovable) arguments about what time it was on each ship, the relative positions they were both in and hugely complex discussions about what coloured lights could be seen from each ship at a given time. In the latter, geometrical diagrams that are more suited to a mathematics degree than a history book appear prominently.

They are academically fascinating no doubt and they underscore a commendable search for truth which is the foundation of all historical study. However, boiled down to their basic principles it is virtually impossible to arrive at a conclusion one way or the other with any confidence. The root of the problem is that there were just a handful of eye-witness accounts surviving from those aboard the *Californian* to act as evidence. They are shot through with contradiction of which the above is just one example.

To be charitable some at least of the key witnesses were mistaken on several key points. To be more cynical, some of them are simply not telling the truth. The nub of the debate is which one, or several, of the witnesses you choose to believe or disbelieve. In the absence of any other evidence, this is – in the tradition of all great courtroom dramas – down to the observers' assessment of the credibility of each witness. Unfortunately, there are some serious questions to be asked of some of the witnesses on both sides of the case, including Captain Lord himself.

A further problem was one that relates directly to the conduct of the investigations that followed the disaster. Both were deeply flawed in terms of their conduct. This does not necessarily mean that they arrived at the wrong conclusion with regards to Captain Lord's inaction. However, it means that in the superficial attitude they took to arrive at that conclusion they did not test the evidence thoroughly. Limited cross-examination of contradictory witnesses was not pursued with appropriate diligence, leaving a number of question marks unresolved.

For the historian this in itself is a tragedy. In the American Inquiry key witnesses were not called. In the British Inquiry contradictions in the accounts of key witnesses were not questioned and probed. In total, because of this amateurish (supporters of Lord would say 'biased') approach much of the evidence that might have helped clear up the debate was not collected. With the passing of time and the death of all the key witnesses there that night, it is now gone forever.

Lord's reaction, when informed of the rocket, or rockets, by Stone was to inform the Second Officer to carry on keeping an eye on the nearby ship and continue his previously unsuccessful attempts to contact her by Morse lamp. Gibson was to be sent down to him with any further information. Lord then went to lay down again, where he soon began to fall into a deep sleep, soothed by the hypnotic sound of the keyboard he could hear being clicked as the Morse lamp sprang into action once again.

Lord said that he had been reassured by his conversation with Stone. He had asked the Second Officer if what he had seen had been company signals, to which Stone had replied that he did not know. However, he took reassurance from the fact that Stone also reported that she had changed her bearing to the south-west which Lord took to mean that the ship was under way and moving further away from the *Californian* (as indeed Stone later confirmed *was* what he meant). This is consistent with what Stone said to Gibson soon after. He took a compass bearing of the ship and told the apprentice: 'She was slowly steering away towards the south-west.'

The arguments around what Lord could and should have done have several dimensions. The first is a pragmatic one; if he had tried to make his way to the *Titanic* could he have arrived in time to make a difference? In the absence of concrete information, his first step would have been to wake up Wireless Operator Evans and ask him to try and find out what was wrong. In a few minutes he would, if he was fortunate, find out of the unfolding disaster on the *Titanic*. He would then have ordered the engines to be started up and made his way towards the ship. Assuming they were not slowed down by any ice (and as he was on the same side of the ice-field as the *Titanic* then that would possibly have been the case though several *Californian* witnesses describe ice to the south of them) he would then have set off towards the *Titanic*.

Let us assume that Lord was indeed first informed of the problem at around 12.45 a.m. *Californian* time (which may as noted have been different from *Titanic* time). Let us assume then that he had found out about the problem via wireless and started the engines at around 1.00 a.m. How far away he actually was from the *Titanic* is of course a matter of great debate. However, taking as yet another assumption that it was 10 miles then that was an hour's steaming away from the ship; it is unlikely to have been any less than that as neither ship could see each other's attempts at Morsing each other and the *Titanic*, the largest ship ever built, would surely have been unmistakable if she had been closer than this distance.

Taking all these best case assumptions, then it would not have been much before 2.00 a.m. before the *Californian* arrived. By then all *Titanic*'s lifeboats had been launched (though some of the collapsibles were still left). Lord could have lowered his own and certainly saved some of those in the water. However, the vast majority of those still on the *Titanic* would have still perished.

The greatest tragedy of all this though is that Lord did not wake up Cyril Evans in an attempt to find out whether there was a ship in distress or not. Lord would later admit to being dissatisfied with Stone's replies about the nature of the rockets but he still chose not to wake up the operator. Supporters of Captain Lord argue that this was because the true power of wireless had yet to be understood. It is not a convincing argument; Lord had already seen fit to send several warning messages that evening using it.

In the meantime, Gibson tried to call the other ship up without any joy. Stone at one stage turned to him and said: 'Look at her now; she looks very queer out of the water; her lights look queer.' Gibson looked at her through his glasses. To him the ship he was looking at seemed to be listing to starboard. Stone then remarked to Gibson that 'a ship was not going to fire rockets at sea for nothing'. The rockets were white and exploded in starbursts. However, there were no explosions to be heard. It was a quiet night. The absence of any explosive sound meant one of two things; either that what they were watching were not distress rockets or that they were being fired from a spot quite a long way off. But they looked just like distress rockets were supposed to look, so that left only the latter explanation.

Gibson carried on watching the ship; her red port side light seemed to be higher out of the water than it had been previously. Stone in the meantime postulated about the ship he could see and what the rockets meant. He concluded that 'there was something the matter with her'. But for whatever reason he was not concerned enough to go and wake his captain up again. He would come across as a very confused witness. He did not believe that the rockets he saw were company signals, yet he did not think they were distress rockets either, so it is not clear just what he thought they might be. As he watched the ship he was sure that she was steaming slowly away and he could not understand why a ship doing that would send up distress rockets. But he also thought that the direction of the rockets was changing in line with the change in direction of the ship he was watching.

Most damning of all this is the vocabulary of the witnesses. Quotes of lights looking 'queer', of ships that appear to be listing, of vessels that look as if there is something the matter with them, suggest something very out of the ordinary. Bear in mind too that the *Californian* was stopped because of the danger posed by an immense ice-field and it is quite incredible that nobody's suspicions were alerted by a series of out-of-the-ordinary indicators in an area of known danger. It is hard to understand how observers from the *Californian* looked on impassively and did nothing.

There was also, to reiterate, no doubt that those on the *Titanic* could see something they thought was a ship from where they were. Pitman in Boat 5 saw a white light on the horizon, which he thought lay on *Titanic*'s track to the west. However, he was not sure what it was and thought that it could have been one of their own lifeboats. He could see no other lights, such as a red side light, and believed that the craft to which the light was attached was stationary. In his view, it was about 3 miles away. He did not think it was a sailing vessel or a steamer; certainly he did not believe that anything was coming to the rescue.

Once they were safely lowered, Jones and the oarsmen in Boat 8 'pulled for the light, but I found that I could not get to it; so I stood by for a while'. Jones was certain that he could not see any children and very few women when he left the ship. He did however notice the Strauses in the vicinity of the boats on deck though he could not hear them speak as steam was blowing from the funnels and the noise was deafening.

There was also a first-class passenger in Boat 8, a woman of rare poise and beauty. This was Noelle, the Countess of Rothes. Born into money with a wealthy landowning father, she had married into it too when she was wed to Norman Leslie, the 19th Earl of Rothes in 1900. The event made the society pages of the best London newspapers and the couple entered easily into the high society of late Victorian and early Edwardian England. As well as socializing, they enjoyed the other facets of contemporary English aristocracy; hunting, boating and riding.

Her husband was no stay at home aristocrat though. Noelle was active in charitable circles but her husband also looked for business opportunities; being a Lord was no guarantee of permanent wealth in these changing times. He travelled widely and in 1912 had gone to Florida to look at the possibilities of making money from a citrus farm. The Countess was now on her way to join him.

A photograph of the Countess taken in 1907 shows a woman of exquisite beauty, a woman of elegance and style rather than sensuousness. In an understated way, Jones – who was in charge of the boat – was also most impressed by her. He noted that 'she was a countess or something' and that 'she had a lot to say so I put her to steering the boat'. This might not sound like much of a compliment but in fact Jones was very taken with the Countess. He would later present her with the brass plate from the boat and they would keep up a correspondence after the disaster.

Also in Boat 8 was the discontented Mrs J. Stuart White. She was disgusted to look up and see stewards smoking cigarettes; what she wondered could be less appropriate at a time like this? But she confirmed the story that an officer (though she didn't name him as Captain Smith) told the boat to row for the lights. In her view, the light was 10 miles away.

She had her cane with an electric light on it which was just as well as the light that had been put in the boat was next to useless. No one seemed panicked or frightened but there was, as she put it, 'a lot of pathos when husbands and wives kissed each other goodbye'. She later claimed that her cane was stolen; Lightoller said that he was so infuriated by 'the damn thing' when she had been waving it around on deck that he had ordered it thrown over the side. It seemed a suitable end to it; in riposte to her questioning as to how appropriate it was to smoke at a time like this, it is difficult not to wonder how appropriate it was to worry about such things at a time like this. Lightoller must have been tempted to throw her in too along with her cane.

It was about 1.10 a.m. when the most controversial boat on the *Titanic* started to lower away. This was Boat Number 1. It was one of the two emergency boats, always swung out ready to be lowered, with a capacity of forty.

Colonel Gracie, a heroic man no doubt but one who saw many aspects of the disaster through rose-tinted spectacles, says that there was no disorder in loading or lowering this boat. This is hardly surprising as there were so few people on it, twelve in all. In addition, the fact that this was the fourth boat from the starboard side and yet it was only just over a quarter full shows how desperately poorly organized the whole loading sequence was. Fifth Officer Lowe later suggested there were twenty-two people in the boat which shows he either had a very poor memory for figures or he was something of a story-teller. With Sir Cosmo Duff Gordon also onboard, a man whose actions would later come under very public scrutiny, this was without doubt the most controversial lifeboat launched that night.

Lookout George Symons had already helped launch Boats 5 and 3 and was then asked to help with Emergency Boat 1. First Officer Murdoch was in charge of loading it. Two women ran out on deck and asked if they could board. Permission was duly granted. There were no more women in sight so the boat was lowered. Just before leaving the Boat Deck, Symons – who had been put in charge – noticed a white light on the port bow about 5 miles away. As they started to pull away from the ship, Symons noticed that the water was now up to C Deck at the bow, coming up to a spot right underneath the ship's name. Symons had been told to lie 100 yards off the *Titanic* and await further orders. He did so for a short time (perhaps quarter of an hour) then pulled further back as he was afraid of the suction when the ship eventually went down.

First-class passenger Charles Stengel, whose wife was already away in a boat, had also climbed in. When he reached the Boat Deck there were no other passengers around and permission was freely given him to get aboard. It was a fair jump from the Titanic to the boat and Stengel tumbled, effectively falling into the boat. Murdoch laughed, saying that this was the funniest sight he had seen all night. Less amusing however was the way that the boat was lowered. The lowering was uneven, the unpractised seaman struggling to co-ordinate their efforts, and the boat almost tipped its occupants into the water far below. Stengel confirmed that Boat 1 later followed a light that could be seen in front of the bows. He personally felt that this was not the light of a ship but merely the Northern Lights reflecting off bergs. However, this was rather a minority assessment. Most people, including a large number of experienced seamen (which Stengel was not) were sure that what they could see was the lights of a ship.

Stengel also seemed to be somewhat embarrassed at his own

personal position. He explained that Boat 1 was nearly full: 'I do not think it had a capacity for any more than were in it.' This was one of the more ludicrous statements of the night, as (to recapitulate) Boat 1 had a capacity of forty and had just twelve people in it. It was perhaps also a feeble attempt by Stengel to explain why this boat, not even half full, did not go back to pick up any more survivors from the water when the boat sank.

He also said that people seemed slow to come up onto the Boat Deck. Whether this was another attempt at self-justification or a more accurate statement which might reflect the fact that people were not being allowed up into a first-class area is not immediately clear. However, most accounts from those in Boat 1 suggest that there were no other passengers waiting to get in when she was lowered which begs the question, where were they?

Sir Cosmo Duff Gordon and his wife Lucy were in it too. They had already tried to get into Boat 7 but that was full by the time they arrived – it was in fact less than half full, but given the cavalier attitude to loading the boats that was prevalent on the Boat Deck that was close enough. They next tried Number 3, where there was enough room for Lady Duff Gordon but not for Sir Cosmo and she would not go without him (though again, this boat was less than two-thirds full).

They asked an officer, presumably Murdoch, if they could get in and he replied that he wished that they would. Lady Duff Gordon later said that she thought she was destined to drown. She had turned down the chance to go in several boats because she would not go without her husband. However, she could see no other passengers waiting to get in the boat. She was now lifted gently into the boat. Safely lowered, the boat began to move slowly away from the wallowing ship. However, Lady Duff Gordon's brush with controversy had only just begun.

Boat 9 was away soon after, also from the starboard side. There were a significant number of second-class passengers on board, all but one of them women, and three single third-class men, who must have shown their initiative to get on the boat deck, possibly by climbing up cranes to get out of their third-class areas.

Boatswain's mate Albert Haines was in her too. He believed that the boat was more or less full when two or three men, presumably the third-class men, jumped into the bow (it is true that the boat was fuller than some, with about fifty people aboard). To him, 'the boat was chock-a-block'. Murdoch told him to stand off, well clear of the ship. They pulled about 100 yards off to a point from where they clearly saw that the *Titanic* was going down by the head.

Quartermaster Walter Wynne was one of seven crew members in the boat. He gave a clear description of the light that could be seen nearby. He could see the lights of a steamer, red at first, then white, about 7–8 miles away. Steward William Ward noticed that Officer Murdoch, Ismay and Purser McElroy were nearby when the boat was being loaded. A sailor got in with a bag and said that he had been instructed to take control of the boat. Haines, who was actually in charge, told him to get out which he duly did. One old lady made a great fuss and refused point-blank to get in. A French lady fell and suffered a minor injury.

In the darkness, the women struggled to gauge the drop from the deck to the boat. Ward was told to get in and help load it. As there were no women left on deck, a few men were allowed to climb aboard. There was some difficulty in laying hold of the oars, as they were tied together and no one had a knife.

James Widgery, a Bath Steward, had seen that a number of passengers were already on deck by the time that he arrived at the boats. He went to Number 7 first but that was already being readied for lowering. He was then sent to Number 9. He confirmed the story about the old lady who would not enter; she was frightened and refused to board.

In the meantime, the illusory hope of that light flickered in the distance, frustratingly not moving any closer to the ship. One of the most detailed accounts of the light came from Able Seaman Edward Buley in Boat 10. He said,

> There was a ship of some description there when she struck, and she passed right by us. We thought she was coming to us; and if she had come to us, everyone could have boarded her. You could see she was a steamer. She had her steamer lights burning. She was off our port bow when we struck, and we started for the same light, and that is what kept the lifeboats together.

He told the American Inquiry that 'I am very positive' that she then stayed stationary for about three hours and then she made tracks. She was only three miles away, he reckoned, and he saw two masthead lights but not her bow light. At one stage they thought she was coming to pick up the lifeboats – 'we saw it going right by us when we were in the lifeboats'.

Unfortunately his statement is rather confusing. He implies that the ship was there when the berg was struck, but if she was then no one else on *Titanic*, including her lookouts, saw her. He says that she was stationary for three hours (which could, loosely applied, implicate the *Californian* though she was actually still for much longer than that) but then makes much of the fact that she seemed to be moving quite significantly, which would definitively rule out *Californian*. Perhaps his choice of words was merely clumsy but if so it is a pity because his statement almost generates more questions than answers.

Seaman Buley had been put in charge of the boat by Chief Officer Wilde. Seaman Frank Evans had also been told to get in by Wilde. William Burke, first-class dining room steward, was also ordered in though he does not say by whom. He had initially gone to Boat 1, which was the boat he had been assigned to. Baker Charles Joughin was putting women and children in the boat. Murdoch was also at hand. There was a 2½ foot gap between the ship and the lifeboat and 'he was catching children by the dresses and chucking them in'.

Joughin recalled Wilde telling the stewards to keep men back, though the order was superfluous as they were doing it anyway. The stewards, firemen and sailors formed orderly lines and passed the women along. They had difficulty finding more women to put in, though Joughin did notice some who would not be parted from their bags. He thinks that the gap to the boat was about 4–5 feet and women had to be dropped into it. He did not himself get into the boat, thinking that that would give a bad example, and instead went back to his room down below to reinforce himself with a drop of liquor.

A woman in a black dress did not jump far enough and was caught between the side of the ship and the lifeboat. She was pulled in by the men on the deck below, returned to the Boat Deck and jumped again, this time successfully. One man (a foreigner) jumped into the lifeboat as it was being lowered. Evans seemed disgusted at his action. The foreigner, possibly Neshan Krekorian, perhaps thought it slightly pointless to stand around waiting to die while half-empty lifeboats rowed away from the doomed leviathan.

Evans however suggested at the American inquiry that the boat was pretty full, which comparatively speaking it was with perhaps fifty-five people in total aboard her. Also in the boat were the Dean family, Ettie, young Bertram and Millvina Dean. However, Bertram senior was left on the ship and was lost. The fate of Millvina was rather different. She would be the last of the survivors to die, passing away on 31 May 2009, exactly ninety-eight years after the *Titanic* was launched.

They rowed away for several hundred yards where they eventually tied up to Boat 12. This had been loaded by Seaman Frederick Clench and Second Officer Lightoller with Chief Officer Wilde passing women and children on to them. There was only one seaman, John Poingdestre, in her when she started to lower away so Wilde told Clench to jump in. They were told to keep an eye on Boat 14 and keep together. Only one male passenger got in, a Frenchman (unnamed) who jumped in as she was being lowered. This might not be heroic but it was certainly rational; there were twenty spare places in the boat. Poingdestre heard Lightoller order the boat to stay close to the ship. They would eventually tie up with collapsible D and three other lifeboats.

Two of the second-class passengers in Boat 12 were Mrs Imanita Shelley and her mother, Mrs Lutie Parrish. One of the sailors had run up to Mrs Shelley, who had been standing on deck, and told her to get into the boat. There was she recalled a 4–5 foot gap to jump. 'The boat was filled with women and children, as many as could get in with overcrowding.' A 'crazed Italian' jumped in, landing on Mrs Parrish and badly bruising her leg. They had been told to head for the boat launched ahead of them. She noticed the men aboard acting in exemplary fashion, putting their clothes around half-dressed women and children.

Poingdestre also noticed a significant change in mood as Boats 12 and 14 were being loaded. Whereas all had been calm before, now passengers were starting to panic. A group of men – he thought that they were second and third-class passengers – began to crowd the boats and Poingdestre and Lightoller only kept them back with difficulty.

Boat 11 was lowered from the starboard side just before half past one. Seaman Walter Brice recalled that the boat was lowered from A Deck. Steward Charles Mackay said that the boat collected the women from the Boat Deck first and then gathered a few more on A Deck. As the boat was then lowered away, the women complained that the boat was so packed they had to stand. They were also unhappy that the men in the boat were smoking. However, the account of Assistant 2nd

Steward Joseph Wheat differed slightly. He also said that Murdoch ordered the boat to be lowered to A Deck but that this was because there no one on the Boat Deck and that was why the boat was lowered down to the deck below.

One of the women in the boat was Edith Russell, who had never felt comfortable on the ship. When a male acquaintance suggested she should get in, she was reluctant as her clothes were so tight she could not climb onto the boat. As she explained, she was 'a prisoner in my own skirts'. However, she was helped on, along with a toy pig covered in white fur that played a tune known as the *Maxixe*.

When an officer asked if there was a sailor onboard, there was no reply so Seaman Brice had climbed out along the falls and lowered himself into the boat. He took over the tiller, by which time the boat had been filled with women and children. There were several problems when the boat was lowered. Firstly, she was nearly swamped by an outflow of water pouring out from the side of the ship. This was the discharge from the pumps that were being worked onboard the Titanic. Then, the ropes snagged.

Quartermaster Sidney Humphreys was in charge. He looked for a light onboard but could find none so he made some improvised torches from lengths of rope. The boat was not very well equipped; Steward McKay was unable to find any compass in the boat when he looked for one.

Steward Ernest Wheelton had previously seen Thomas Andrews looking into rooms to see if there was anyone there. When he arrived on deck, Boats 7, 5 and 9 had gone and Number 11 was already in the davits. Murdoch ordered him in. When the boat was almost full, Murdoch asked if there were any sailors in the boat. When the answer was in the negative, two climbed in (including the aforementioned Brice). Wheelton also confirmed that the boat was lowered from A Deck.

The stories so far are of passengers standing by the boats, patiently waiting their turn or resigning themselves to their fate. However, there are other stories to tell that cannot be fully told for the simple reason that most of the people who need to tell them did not survive. Hundreds of people were still nowhere near the Boat Deck and their tale can only be told by frustratingly but inevitably incomplete titbits of information.

Gathered some way away from the Boat Deck with his small group, Olaus Abelseth and his companions were among those who heard an officer say that they should be quick, for there was a boat coming. Abelseth still did not have his lifejacket and went back down below to pick it up. When he returned, he saw a lot of steerage passengers using cranes as makeshift ladders from the steerage open area up onto the Boat Deck. There was no other way, for the gates allowing access via more conventional means were locked. Yet both Inquiries would later insist that there was no discrimination by class; one of the more unsustainable conclusions of two unsatisfactory Inquiries.

To these poor souls, any hope of survival was receding rapidly. Steward Hart, an unsung hero, had been doing his job as well as he was able and escorting groups of steerage women and children up to the boats but he was on his own in his efforts. Most other third-class passengers seemed to have been left to their own devices. Any hope of survival rested either on their own initiative or on plain old-fashioned luck. The men would not heroically give up their places to the women and children here. Most of them would have no say in the matter. By now, the majority of those in third-class had already been condemned to a watery grave. And the moment at which they would look with terror into the dark abyss of their destiny was now less than an hour away.

6

Nowhere to Go

01.31–02.00, 15 April 1912

The real horror of the *Titanic* disaster was the sheer drawn-out nature of the ship's death. It was only by degrees that the true magnitude of the pending disaster revealed itself to those on deck or down below. The gradual tipping of the ship as the bows sank lower beneath the waves and the angle of the stern rose correspondingly higher, and the listing of the ship to port or starboard (both seem to have happened at some stage during the two hours and forty minutes it took for the ship to go down) began to tell its own tale. Now a new terror was about to emerge; the lifeboats were about to run out.

The fact that there were not enough places for all onboard would soon become apparent but it was certainly clearer now to the officers loading the boats who started to fill them with many more passengers than were on the earlier boats. It was an awful situation, the horror of which was now fully dawning on those on the ship. Before long, over 1,500 of them would have nowhere to go.

Boat 14 was one of the next to be lowered, with about sixty people in her. Seaman Joseph Scarrott was initially put in charge of the boat, his bad vibes about the ship that he had felt back in Southampton now fully justified. Some men tried to rush the boat, 'foreigners' as he described them. Discipline was beginning to break down now that the urgency of the situation was more apparent. One man had to be thrown out three times. Fifth Officer Lowe came along and Scarrott briefed him on the problems he was experiencing. Lowe took hold of his revolver and decided to take charge of what was a deteriorating situation.

Seaman Scarrott told how 'half a dozen foreigners' tried to jump in when there were still women and children to be loaded but he beat them off with the tiller. When Scarrott told Lowe what had happened, he took out his pistol, a Browning automatic. The tension was now palpable and a sense of panic was becoming increasingly evident. Lowe fired shots down into the water as a warning against any attempt that others might make to enter the boats when they were not allowed to. Greaser Frederick Scott was watching on and thought he heard him say: 'If any man jumps into the boat I will shoot him like a dog.'

Lowe believed that the boat was crowded to capacity and might buckle under the weight. He saw a lot of 'Latin people', like 'wild beasts' waiting to jump in as the boat as she was lowered down the side of the stricken ship. Lowe fired several shots (Scarrott remembered two, Lowe reckoned three) from his pistol to keep the crowd back, taking care to fire into the gap between the boat and the side of the ship so that no one was hit.

Lowe had been looking after the lowering of Numbers 12, 14 and 16, which were all put down at more or less the same time. Sixth Officer Moody suggested that Lowe should get in Boat 14 and take charge of the small flotilla. Lowe agreed and climbed in. Two men tried to jump in and Lowe chased them out. Lowe filled Boat 14 and Moody Boat 16 with women and children; Lightoller was also in the vicinity part of the time. One man, an 'Italian' it was suggested, dressed as a woman in a shawl and crept in the boat. Another man, Charles Williams (a second-class passenger), was asked by Lowe to get in to row (this contradicts Colonel Gracie who said that only one male passenger got off on this side).

Charlotte Collyer and her young daughter were here too. Boat 14 was about half full when someone grabbed young Madge from Charlotte Collyer's arms and threw her in a boat. So sudden was the move that she did not even have time to say goodbye to her father. Charlotte clung desperately to her husband even as the deck slanted more steeply beneath her feet. She did not want to leave Harvey but she did not wish to abandon Madge either, leaving her with an agonizing decision to make. Two men virtually ripped her from her husband's arms and dragged her away. Harvey urged her to be brave and told her that he would get off in another boat. Whilst not everybody on board the *Titanic* acted heroically, some certainly did.

Charlotte was hurled bodily into the boat, landing on her shoulder and bruising it badly. As other women were waiting to get on behind her, she looked over their heads, seeking a last view of her beloved Harvey. All she saw was his back, as he walked away from the boat towards the other men. At the last, Officer Lowe jumped in and ordered the boat lowered away. Then a young lad climbed into it, barely more than a schoolboy. He fell among the women and crawled under a seat.

The women wanted to save him but Lowe would not have it. The Officer drew his pistol and threatened to blow his brains out. This only made the lad beg for his life, so Lowe tried a different tack. 'For God's sake, be a man, we have got women and children,' he simply said. Madge took Lowe's hand and begged him not to shoot the youth. The Officer smiled and the youth regained his composure and climbed back aboard the ship. There was barely a dry eye in the boat. Quite what it proved though is not clear. There was not a lot of room left but room there was and one more person aboard would not have sunk her. There were no more women and children on the spot to enter the boat anyway.

Eva Hart and her mother were put into Boat 14 without too much trouble. Eva bade farewell to her father, though she did not understand what was happening. He told her to hold her mummy's hand and be a good girl. Then the boat was lowered away. Eva was understandably terrified. She would never see her father again and the events of that night were to give her nightmares for years. Hers was one of many poignant farewells to be said on that cold and terrifying night.

Also off in Boat 14 was Edith Brown. She, like many others, had seen the lights of another ship from the Boat Deck, however the lights seemed at some stage to go out. She recalled being able to see the ice for miles around. She said that a number of her fellow passengers felt that the ship was unsinkable so had gone back to bed after the berg was struck even though there were ice fragments on the ship.

Edith's father had been the picture of calmness on the ship, saying nothing of the seriousness of the disaster and smoking on a cigar. After he put his wife and daughter in the boat, he simply walked away. It was not until Edith was on the water that she could see how the ship was sinking as the lights slowly slipped under the waves.

Charlotte Collyer told how, as the boat was on its way down, a steerage passenger, almost inevitably an 'Italian' according to Charlotte, leapt in. He fell upon a young child, injuring her. Lowe caught hold of him and flung him back on deck. As the boat continued its downward motion, Charlotte looked up and saw the 'Italian' being beaten to a pulp. Eventually the boat hit the water with a thud and prepared to move off.

Charlotte's evidence, like that of many others, is suspect in places. She says that when the boat reached the water those aboard could see the berg that had hit them for the first time, yet most survivors suggest that the sight of the ice was a shock when the sun first came up so she was certainly capable of embellishing a story. It is difficult to separate fact from fiction and the best that can be done is to seek corroborating details from other sources.

Some of the accounts come across as being dramatized and stereotyped, such as Charlotte's 'Italian'. Charlotte would also lose a beloved husband and the conduct of a coward made Harvey Collyer's undoubted heroism even more heroic in comparison. It does not mean that such things did not happen, just that much of what has been written, often in all probability in good faith, needs to be interpreted with caution.

About 5 feet from the surface of the water, the tackle got tangled and the boat had to be cut free. Steward George Crowe who was in the boat had also feared that she would be rushed by a crowd, 'probably Italians, or some foreign nationality other than English or American' as he jarringly described them (all these accusations against Italians would later prompt a complaint from the Italian Ambassador and an apology from Fifth Officer Lowe).

Crowe also heard the pistol shots fired by Lowe but was sure that no one was hurt. They did however succeed in stopping the rush. Apart from a woman crying, there was little disturbance. Not long after reaching the water, the boat seemed to have sprung a leak and several onboard had to start bailing her out. Some of the men used their hats to do this, a rather nice symbolic summation of some of the organization onboard the *Titanic* that night.

Miss Sarah Compton, a first-class passenger, could not even see the boat when it was her turn to board. She was virtually thrown into it. This was the general experience of the women who found it difficult to climb into the boats. She noticed that it proved difficult and jerky to lower the boats. Boat 14 eventually struck the water very hard. Once they were safely on the sea, they rowed about 150 yards away, holding their position close to the *Titanic*. The boat later tied up with Boats 4, 10, 12 and Collapsible D.

Boat 16 went away on the port side soon after. Able Seaman Ernest Archer said that everything was still quiet when the boats were being loaded. Young Steward Charles Andrews, just nineteen years of age, witnessed the fact that no steerage men were allowed in, having being told by the 'officer' loading the boat not to allow it. She went away with fifty-six people in her, pretty full but still with nine spare places. One of those on the boat was Karen Abelseth, sister of Olaus.

Olaus Abelseth and his group had been clustered towards the stern of the ship. Eventually, an officer came and shouted for the women to make their way forward. The gates were opened and Abelseth's two female companions were allowed through. However, the men were to stay where they were for the time being.

Archer still did not think the ship was doomed: 'To tell you the truth, I did not think the ship would go down. I thought we might go back to her again afterwards.' Steward Andrews was so convinced that he could see a light behind the sinking ship that he thought it was a vessel coming to the rescue.

Also in Number 16 was Stewardess Violet Jessop who noted that the crowd parted to let through a large crowd of third-class passengers, mainly foreigners, in. They rushed to the boat and for a moment it seemed as if there would be a breakdown in order. However, the officer in charge of loading regained control and the boat was lowered. But it was lowered in a jerky fashion, tipping first one way and then the other, threatening to deposit its passengers in the water far below.

As Violet got in, a baby was put in her arms. As the boat made her way down the side of the ship, it passed decks where lights still burned brightly through the portholes, illuminating the boat in searing rays of light before it disappeared again into the darkness. As she looked up, she saw people looking over the decks at them. Then, the boat hit the water with a crunching thud, which alarmed the baby and set if off crying. Someone shouted out an order for the men in the boat to row and the few there set to it. Violet noticed one of them, a stoker, dressed only in a thin singlet to keep him warm. He was still blackened with coal dust and his eyes were red from working with the furnaces. He took a cigarette from his pocket and started smoking it after offering Violet half of it.

Violet recalled that she had always wanted to see *Titanic* from a distance to appreciate fully her size and splendour. Now, in these other-worldly circumstances, the chance had unexpectedly arrived.

It was, as she later described it, an incredible sight: 'My *Titanic*, magnificent queen of the ocean, a perfection of man's handiwork, her splendid lines outlined against the night, every light twinkling.' And yet as she continued to gaze fascinated at the ship, something incredible was happening. She counted the lines of light that blazed from her deck by deck. She counted to six. Looking a few minutes later, she saw only five, then four. There was no doubt about it, despite her shocked incredulity. The *Titanic* was sinking.

The women in the boat started to weep, quietly in the main, overwrought by the immensity of the horror unfolding before them of which they were front-row observers. Now more in hope than expectation, Violet scanned the horizon once more for the lights of the ship they had seen. She should be getting nearer now but she was sure that they were in fact further away. It was now clear that there would be no last minute reprieve from this direction.

Leading Stoker Fred Barrett had now arrived on A Deck, where only boats 13 and 15 were left. The two were lowered more or less together (this evidence contradicts the British Inquiry times noted by Gracie which suggests they were lowered ten minutes apart). The fall in Boat 13, the first to be lowered, had to be cut by Barrett, only just in time as Boat 15 was almost on top of her by this time. Barrett took charge but was overcome by the cold. Someone covered him with a blanket to help him warm up.

Dr Washington Dodge confirmed that Boats 13 and 15 were put in the davits at about the same time. He overheard an officer say that they would lower them from A Deck. He saw a group of around sixty people gathered around Boat 15 and decided to make his way down to A Deck. There were only about eight women there he later recalled. In fact he was mistaken; over twenty women got aboard. Dr Dodge, along with many other male survivors it seems, wished to justify his ongoing existence by suggesting that it would have been a futile waste of a life to stay aboard when there was plenty of room to go (a perfectly natural thing to do when there was space in the boats to do so). He was lucky; Steward Frederick Ray, who looked after him onboard the *Titanic*, was one of those in the vicinity and told him to get in.

Steward Ray recalled there was a fat lady who did not want to get into the boat. The size of the tiny craft when set against the magnitude of the vast sea was terrifying. However, she was given little option and was put onboard. A baby, wrapped in a blanket, was handed to someone in the boat, to be followed in by the woman carrying it. As they were lowered, they left three or four men by the deck rail. Ray saw them moving towards Boat Number 15.

More third-class passengers were reaching the Boat Deck, only now there were hardly any boats remaining. Daniel Buckley was one of those now crowded around, with things now clearly desperate and likely to become more so. When Boat 13 was being lowered, a large number of men rushed her, including Buckley. The officers forced them out, firing shots in the air to drive them off according to him, replacing them with a mixed group of steerage passengers. Buckley, crying through fear, however managed to remain in it. A woman had thrown her shawl over him and disguised him. He thought it was Mrs Astor but this was wishful thinking; she would be in Boat 4.

Even now, some passengers were more terrified at being adrift in an open boat than they were of remaining on the *Titanic*. A woman in Buckley's boat, Bridget Bradley, got in, thought better of it, and tried to get out again. Fortunately for her, one of the sailors pulled her back in and the boat was then lowered away with her still in it.

As Boat 13 was being lowered, Lawrence Beesley looked over the side and saw that it was now level with the rail of B Deck. It appeared fairly full to him. There was a shout for more ladies to make their way to the boat but no reply. One of the crew looked up to Beesley, on the deck above, and asked if there were any more ladies on his deck. When the reply was in the negative, the friendly voice then suggested that Beesley should jump in. He sat on the edge of the deck and dangled his legs over the side. Throwing his dressing gown, which he had draped over his arm, into the boat first of all Beesley then jumped.

Almost as he landed, there was a shout that there were more women on B Deck. Two ladies were then passed over into the dangling lifeboat. Their story was revealing. They told Beesley that they had been on a lower deck and had climbed up to B Deck not by the normal stairway but up an iron ladder used by the crew. Other ladies had been in front of them but one of them was a large woman and her progress had been slow. Quite why women, presumably third-class (there were eighteen of them in this boat), had to climb iron ladders to reach the boats is something of a mystery and poses some intriguing and uncomfortable questions for those who believed there was no class discrimination in play.

Then, just as the boat was being lowered away, a family appeared on deck, husband, wife and baby. The baby was handed to a lady at the stern and the mother got into the middle of the boat. The father jumped in as the boat was being lowered. The only family fitting this description in Boat 13 were the Caldwell's, second-class passengers from Illinois. Boat 13 was lowered slowly and jerkily down the side of the *Titanic*. Its occupants looked bewilderedly through cabin windows whose lights still burned brightly.

As they neared the water, someone noticed the pump discharge. There was a hole 2 feet wide and a foot deep with a large volume of water pouring out. They shouted up to those lowering the boat to stop at once, fearing they would be swamped. Fortunately, their shouts were heard and the lowering was halted. Now they used the oars to push themselves away from the side of the ship and the discharge that threatened to deluge them. However, no one onboard knew how to release them from the tackle that had been used to lower them so they had to cut themselves free.

Now in the water, they had started to drift along the side of the boat. A serious situation was quickly developing for Boat 15 was being lowered on top of them. When it was only two feet above them, they shouted up for those lowering the latter to stop. In the nick of time, they did so. Boat 15 dangled there while Barrett cut the rope.

Dr Dodge found it was difficult to get hold of the oars. They had been tied together with heavily tarred twine. In addition, they had been placed in a spot where they were difficult to access, beneath the seats in which the occupants sat. He wondered at the attitude of those sitting on them, who did not seem inclined to move themselves so that the oars could be reached. With difficulty, the oars were at last put in position and used to push the boat away from the side of the ship.

The boat was once more poorly prepared. There were no lights onboard and those tasked with rowing were ill-equipped for the task. They headed for a lifeboat that was carrying a light but, although it only appeared to be a quarter of a mile away, they never managed to reach it.

When the boat started to pull away from the ship, it was realized that there was no one in it who was an obvious candidate to command her. Eventually a stoker was nominated for the dubious honour. It was decided that they should stay close to other boats. Those in the boat appeared to know that help was on its way but believed that it was from the *Olympic*. They too saw a light and rowed towards it, two lights, one above the other but as hard as they rowed they were unable to make any progress towards it. The lights in the end drew away and then disappeared altogether.

However, that was as yet in the future, for at the moment what grabbed their attention was the unbelievable sight of the *Titanic*. The scene was a dramatic one. The sky was without a cloud and the stars shone with rare brilliance. So thickly were they clustered that there seemed to be more stars than black sky that night. Then there was the intense, bitter cold. There was hardly a breath of wind, just a cold, motionless chill that froze those in the boat to the bone. The sea was the third element of this trinity. It was calmer than any of the seamen aboard ever remembered it. One said that it reminded him of a picnic, so flat and waveless was it.

But these were just the backdrop. The great ship itself dominated the view from Boat 13, still close at hand. She stood quietly, almost as if she had accepted her fate. She sank ever so slowly deeper into the sea. Beesley thought her like a wounded animal. Her massive bulk dominated the view. Her black outline stood silhouetted against the sky and the stars. She looked beautiful save for one thing. She was still brightly lit but the lines of lights were slanting at increasingly crazy angles.

Boat 15 was also initially loaded on the Boat Deck and then taken down to A Deck to pick up a few more passengers. It is symptomatic of the confused evacuation techniques in use that there did not even seem to be a clear idea of where the boats should be loaded from. The boat was then taken down to B Deck, where there were far more people waiting to board. Fireman George Cavell believed that about sixty people were put in from this lower deck and that there were about seventy in total aboard her when she was lowered. He thought most of the female passengers who boarded were 'Irish girls'.

Fireman William Taylor insisted later that he had been assigned to Boat 15 all along and that is where he made his way. Although he and the crew got in on the Boat Deck, the lifeboat was then lowered down to A and then B Deck to fill her up. Most of the passengers loaded here he thought were steerage including a number of women and children. He looked around and could see no others left, though there was a large crowd of men. Boat 15, in common with many others, then started to head for the light of a ship.

Steward Rule said that about six men were put in on the Boat Deck and she was then lowered to A and B Deck. By now, there was a slight list to port. Scouts were sent along the deck to look for more women and children; there were none. There was then a rush when men were asked to step aboard. There were not enough places to go around and a number were left standing where they were.

Steward John Stewart was in this boat too. He may have been the last person to see Thomas Andrews alive. He saw him in the otherwise empty Smoking Room as the end approached, staring blankly at the picture of Plymouth Harbour. His lifejacket was lying on the table. When Stewart asked him if he was going to make a try for it, he did not even bother to reply. Boat 15 got away about three quarters of an hour before the ship went down so stories that have Andrews still in the Smoking Room at the very end may or may not be true.

By this time, Hart had arrived with another party of third-class passengers. Boat 15 was the only one left on the starboard side; a large number of third-class passengers had got off in Boat 13, presumably the party he had escorted up before. Boat 15 was filled with Hart's passengers. However, there is some confusion in his account. He suggests that most of the loading took place on the Boat Deck which contradicts Cavell's evidence previously quoted. He says that only ten further people, including a man with a baby in his arms, entered from A Deck. Hart was then ordered into the boat by First Officer Murdoch. He perhaps deserved his place in the boats more than most given his efforts in saving some at least of the third-class passengers.

Hart also saw some women and children left but intimated that they remained on the ship by choice as frequent requests for more women and children were made and none responded. Hart stated that no women were stopped from entering the boats. He could still see a masthead light from the Boat Deck as Boat 15 was lowered. He confirmed that the stewards as a group did their best in helping third-class to the boats; however, the evidence suggests that he alone took the initiative in doing this.

Apart from the collapsibles there were only two boats now left on the *Titanic*, Numbers 2 and 4. Number 2 was an emergency boat, capable of carrying forty people in her. Despite the situation, incredibly there would still be room for fifteen more in her by the time that she was lowered. One of those who got off in Number 2 was Miss Elizabeth Allen. She said that while she was on the deck waiting to get on a boat she did not hear the band once. A line of men, about eighteen long, 'officers' as she described them, got in and were ordered back out again by an officer who called them all cowards.

However, apart from a couple of pathos-ridden goodbyes, there was no panic.

Even as Boats 2 and 4 were prepared, Collapsible D was also being got ready to be slotted into the davits once they were free. Some of those in Boat 2 did not speak English; these presumably included the Kink family from Switzerland. The loading was directed by First Officer Murdoch. As the boat was being filled, Able Seaman Frank Osman saw several steerage passengers come up to the Boat Deck. The men, steerage as well as others, stood back while the women and children got in and there was still no panic. However, there were other accounts stating that Lightoller had to order several men out of the boat with the aid of a pistol (which was not loaded).

The boat was lowered away. It only had to travel some 15 feet to the water rather than the 70 feet that would normally be the case. Someone shouted to the lifeboats from the ship through a megaphone, telling them to row around to the starboard side; this may well have been Captain Smith as he was seen with a megaphone elsewhere that night. Boxhall rowed around, thinking he could take off maybe another three people. However, when he got about 22 yards off the ship he felt a little suction and feared that the boat might be pulled under if the Titanic sank. He was also disturbed by the number of people still on the ship looking to get on a lifeboat and he was afraid that his small craft would be overwhelmed.

Boxhall did manage to find a box of rockets which they had loaded thinking mistakenly that they were biscuits. They would prove useful later when the *Carpathia* was heading towards them. He did not steer for the light as, according to Osman, he was not sure if it was there or not. Osman however believed that it was and that it was sailing away from them. Perhaps Boxhall, who had for an hour and more being trying to Morse the ship and attract her attention with his rockets, had given her up as a lost cause. But Steward James Johnston was in the boat too and was convinced that he saw the white and red lights of a ship away in the distance.

By now, Boat 4 was the only lifeboat, other than the collapsibles, left to lower. Mrs Martha Stephenson noticed that on returning to A Deck again the lights were still on. The boats were lowered parallel to the window and deck-chairs formed a precarious bridge across the gap. With the list now worsening, some men felt that the women would not be able to make it across. A ladder was called for but before it arrived the women were in. Mrs Stephenson found it quite easy to jump across. She saw Colonel Astor saying goodbye to Madeleine and asking what boat they were in. There were some blankets thrown into the boat, which later proved invaluable. Every woman on the deck at that time was taken off.

Colonel Gracie personally carried Mrs Astor over the 4-foot rail. He then heard J.J. Astor ask Lightoller for permission to enter – he explained that she was 'in a delicate position' because of her pregnancy – but the officer refused while there were still any women and children left onboard. Lightoller recalled the conversation in which Astor asked for the boat number; he thought that he might be the subject of a complaint at a later stage.

Mrs Ryerson also got on the boat. Her boy Jack was with her. When an officer tried to stop him getting into the boat, her husband argued the point (young Jack was only thirteen) and won. Mrs Ryerson then turned and kissed her husband who was standing with Mr Thayer and others very quietly. Mrs Ryerson fell in the boat and scrambled across others onboard to the bows of the boat. An officer checked how many women were aboard; the reply twenty-four was shouted back. Mrs Ryerson watched: 'the ropes seemed to stick at one end. Someone called for a knife, but it was not needed until we got in the water as it was but a short distance; and then I realised for the first time how far the ship had sunk.' The deck was only about 20 feet from the sea. She could see 'all the portholes open' (which would not have helped the ship stay afloat for any longer) and the sea pouring in through them. The decks were still lit.

There was only one seaman in the boat so the cry for more went up and several men ('not sailors' according to Mrs Ryerson) climbed down into the boat. Someone shouted to the boat to go to the gangway, where presumably more people might be taken off. By this stage, barrels and chairs were being thrown overboard for use as impromptu rafts. Few were in doubt now that the great ship, pride of the White Star fleet, was soon to plummet to the ocean depths.

Quartermaster Walter Perkis lowered the boat and walked aft. However, then someone called out for another man in the boat so he slid down the lifeline from the davits into it and then took command.

Greaser Frederick Scott had gone to the starboard side but could see no boats there. Going to the port side, he heard a shot and an officer, presumably Lowe, shouting that if any man approached a boat without his permission he would 'shoot him like a dog'. Boat 4 laid off close to the ship. Scott tried to climb down a rope into her but fell in the water, where he was picked up. He recalls the time as being nearly 2.00 a.m. Greaser Thomas Granger would also be picked up in much the same way.

With no lifeboats left, now was the time to start launching the collapsibles. The first of them to be lowered was Collapsible C. It was obvious as the ship lurched lower and the boats were now nearly all gone that the situation was becoming parlous. By now a circle had been formed around the boats and only women were being let through. Quartermaster George Rowe was in charge of her. Chief Officer Wilde wanted a sailor and Captain Smith ordered Rowe to get in. A pantryman, Albert Pearce, entered the boat carrying two babies under his arms.

The collapsible had a nominal capacity of forty-seven and would be lowered with about forty people in her. However, another controversial incident was about to occur. Bruce Ismay had been around the lifeboats from the very beginning and had played an active part in the loading of them. Now, the boat was about to be lowered, one of the last left, and there was a space in it. He looked around for other people to go but could see none (which again begs the question where were they then?). Just as the boat was about to be lowered, Ismay stepped in. Perhaps he was unnerved; he had certainly felt the sensation of the ship sinking under him and could see that she was going down by the head.

The story of Ismay's entry into the boat is one of the great controversies of the disaster and Rowe was an up-close witness to it. Chief Officer Wilde asked if there were any more women or children to be loaded but no one replied or stepped forward. Rowe could not see any, nor for that matter could he see any men on the Boat Deck. He was fairly certain that Wilde did not suggest to either Ismay or fellow first-class passenger William Carter that they enter the boat though, and intimated that they took the decision for themselves. Ismay explained his decision by saying merely that there was a place in the boat and there was no one else around to fill it.

However, he took no measures to enquire whether any steps had been taken to find anyone else on the ship who could get in, though as the boat was already being lowered it was presumably too late for this anyway. Yet Ismay also admitted to Sir Robert Finlay, appearing at the British enquiry on behalf of the White Star Line, that he knew there must have been others left aboard who had not yet got in a boat, and would not do so. At the last moment, he opted to become a passenger rather than the Managing Director of the White Star Line. Whatever the rights or wrongs of his decision, it was one that would haunt him for the rest of his days.

Rowe could see a bright light about 5 miles away, two points off the port bow; he thought it was a sailing ship. He only noticed it after he got into the boat. As it was lowered, the *Titanic* was listing 6 degrees to port. The collapsible kept bumping the ship's prominent rivets as it was lowered, and Rowe had trouble keeping it away from the side. Because of the rubbing, it took a good five minutes to reach the sea. They then rowed towards the bright light – Ismay recalled this too in his later evidence – but made no progress towards it (Rowe believed that it was a white stern light), so in the end they turned around and headed for the green light of another lifeboat.

There were still over 1,500 people left on the ship, a number of them from third-class. The fate of third-class passengers was often a grim one and for them more than any other class (except for second-class men, who statistically suffered more deaths than any other category of passenger in percentage terms) the odds of survival were stacked against them. For once, absolute statistics do not tell the whole story. Of the third-class passengers 177 did survive but nearly 70 of these were on the collapsibles, the last boats to leave (two of which were not launched properly).

Twenty-eight also got off in Boat 13 and 38 in Boat 15, both of which owed much to the dutiful attentions of Steward Hart who led groups of third-class passengers through the rabbit-warren of passageways up to the Boat Deck. This left just thirty-seven in the other fourteen boats, many of which survived purely down to their own resourcefulness and a wise inability to do as they were told.

Edward Ryan from County Tipperary was one example of a man who survived because he used his wits. He wrote to his parents in May 1912 that he had a towel around his neck as he stood on the deck. He threw this over his head and let it hang at the back. His waterproof raincoat also helped disguise him. He walked stiffly past the officers who simply did not bother to look at him thinking that he was a woman. He got off in Boat 14. Although his actions may not seem very heroic, he perhaps thought that as there was room for more people in the boat, it seemed a bit pointless just to hang around to die.

There was also evidence, though few bothered to look for it

very hard at the time, that third-class passengers had been forcibly restrained below decks until it was too late for them to escape. A young seventeen-year-old, Kathy Gilnagh, reported that she was held back with her friends by a barrier manned by a seaman. It was only when James Farrell, another third-class passenger, yelled at him that he meekly relented.

Another third-class colleen, Annie Kelly, stated later that the staircases up from third-class were blocked for fear that the passengers would overwhelm the boats. They were stopped from coming up until the last moment, though Annie survived because a friendly steward made a point of leading her up to the Boat Deck.

Margaret Murphy, also in steerage, was quoted in the *Irish Independent* of 9 May as saying that the doors were locked leading up from third-class. Male passengers in particular were shouting and swearing at the sailors and scuffles broke out. Women and children were praying and crying, terrified at the dreadful fate that loomed. Some of the sailors then battened down the hatches, saying that by trapping air below decks the ship would stay afloat for longer. All this contrasts markedly with the mythology that soon developed which suggested that passengers meekly hung around waiting to die with an air of calm resignation.

Seaman John Poingdestre saw an estimated 100 men waiting with baggage beside a ladder to second-class which was blocked by stewards. Charlotte Collyer saw guards being posted to stop more passengers from coming up on deck. All in all, there is not only evidence that third-class passengers were disadvantaged, the evidence that exists is compelling and conclusive.

Olaus Abelseth was still trapped towards the stern as the ship dipped lower. The women had been gone for some time before there was a shout for 'everybody'. However, by the time Abelseth, his brother-in-law and his cousin eventually got onto the Boat Deck it lacked many boats. On the port side, the last boat was being lowered so they moved over to starboard. Here, an officer was looking for sailors to man a boat. Abelseth had been a fisherman for six years but said nothing because his companions did not want him to go. He stayed where he was, his position increasingly precarious.

Some tragic stories were later reported concerning the steerage passengers. Catherine Buckley had been persuaded by her sister Margaret to join her in America where she had already settled. Her parents did not want her to go. She was lost and when Margaret later turned up at her parents' home, the door was slammed in her face amid accusations that she was a murderess.

Denis Lennon and Mary Mullin, also from Ireland, had fallen in love and eloped together. Realizing where they were headed, Mary's brother, Joe, set off after them and only just missed them as the tender carried them out to the *Titanic* in Queenstown Harbour. He hammered the barrier keeping him back from the departing *Titanic* as she left Queenstown in frustration, an emotion that turned to something rather stronger when news came that both had been lost in the disaster.

Jack Thayer, still aboard, noticed that there was now an increasing sense of panic. A number of men were competing for the few places left but he could see no women waiting to get on. He watched as Bruce Ismay stepped into the last boat to be lowered. He was still a very young man and felt understandable pangs of regret that he was going to be deprived of so much of his life.

Jack Thayer and Milton Long now debated whether or not to try and get into one of the last boats. The ship was clearly sinking by the head, though her rate of submersion was still quite slow. However, the sense of panic was now strong and they felt that the boats would certainly be overturned in the chaos they felt was imminent. They watched in horror as one boat that was being lowered stuck on one side and almost tipped its occupants out. They shouted out for the lowering to be stopped and it was. The boat at last reached the water safely.

Thayer and Long now believed that the last boat had gone, being unaware of the collapsibles still left onboard. They discussed how best to survive. Thayer wanted to climb out on one of the lifeboat falls, scramble down the ropes and swim out to one of the boats. They were still about 60 feet above the water, too far to jump without a serious risk of knocking themselves out or killing themselves. They walked up some stairs on the starboard side, quietly sending messages to their families in their prayers.

Second Officer Lightoller was also left aboard. He kept going to look at the emergency stairs to gauge how quickly the *Titanic* was sinking. It was now obvious that not only was she going but she was going very soon. It would be unforgivable if she should sink with any boats left aboard; time was of the essence in loading them.

On his way back to the boats, he met a party of the officers, one of whom, a Junior Surgeon, smiled at him and asked 'Hello Lights, are you warm?' Despite the coldness of the night Lightoller had taken off his coat and was working so hard that the sweat was pouring off him. He bade the officers goodbye and then returned to the boats, determined to offload them as quickly as possible.

With just collapsibles left to worry about, Lightoller now met the engineers coming up from below. They had been released from duty a while back but had stuck to their posts even when they could no longer do much good in anything save a moral sense. In theory, they all had an allotted place in the boats. In practice, as Lightoller himself admitted, this was a farce with insufficient space for less than half the people onboard. There were many alleged heroes onboard ship that night, some deserving of the attribute, others less so. Every single engineer onboard the *Titanic* that night was lost. The roll call of the lost is a fitting indicator of the heroism of the engineers aboard, a sacrifice that was commemorated with a magnificent memorial in Southampton after the event.

Those already safely off in the boats now stood off to the side, unsure what to do. In Boat 3, with Elizabeth Shute aboard, the tendency of those aboard was at first to stay close to the *Titanic*. Her great bulk provided a misleading reassurance. However, the mirage of security was increasingly appearing misplaced. The bows of the ship were dipping ever lower in the water, her profile becoming portentously darker as lights disappeared under the water. They looked in vain for a light to assist them in the boat but found nothing. Neither were there any biscuits for sustenance nor any water. The boat was completely unprepared for the crisis, and if a rescue ship did not appear quickly then the prospects for those who survived the initial disaster did not look good.

Messages for help had gone out and been answered. The *Mount Temple* had picked up a message from the *Titanic* to the *Olympic* saying that her engine rooms had flooded. Captain Haddock had replied 'am lighting up all possible boilers as fast as I can'. Sadly for all aboard the *Titanic*, he was too far away to make any difference. To the south, perhaps still 30 miles away, the *Carpathia* was going as fast as she could. It would be several hours before she arrived.

The desperateness of the situation was felt equally by most of those in the lifeboats. Most of them could not find any provisions even if they were in fact there. They had seen no sign of a rescue ship other than the illusory light of a distant vessel that did not seem to be doing anything to help them. It was a terrible situation to be in. However, it was preferable even then to that of those left on the ship, sagging every lower in the water, her lights still burning but now burrowing down deeper into the ocean. Time was evidently running out.

7

Waiting for Oblivion

02.01–02.17, 15 April 1912

It was 2.05 a.m. There were now about 1,600 people left aboard the *Titanic*. There were three collapsible boats yet to be launched with a capacity of slightly less than 150. The odds against survival were now stacked against those who had not got off the ship which was dipping lower and lower into the ocean.

That was not all. The *Titanic*'s builders had thought of most things; Turkish baths, swimming pools, gymnasiums, elevators. Thomas Andrews had earlier, in a very different world, made a mental note to attend to some of the smallest details that were wrong when he returned to Belfast, including the design of the ship's coat-hooks. Given all this attention to detail, it was unfortunate that nobody had bothered to put two of the three remaining collapsibles in a place from where they could easily be launched.

Dotted around the *Titanic*, those in the lifeboats looked back towards the stricken ship, the centre of their universe. Boat 14, with Charlotte Collyer aboard, moved away from the *Titanic* and stopped perhaps half a mile away. Charlotte looked back and saw the ship looking 'like an enormous glow worm'. The lights were still burning brightly, illuminating both the decks and the cabins. The only sound that reached her was that of the band playing a lively ragtime number. Although she could not make out any details, she could see clumps of passengers huddling together on deck. The whole scene was one of terrible beauty, made worse by the fact that her beloved Harvey was still somewhere onboard.

The band had had a busy night. Purser McElroy had ordered all the musicians to assemble around midnight. They had started to play in the A Deck lounge where there was a piano; obviously, only one of the pianists could have played. They were later asked to move to the Boat Deck lobby by the main stairs. An upright piano was located there, so one of the pianists could have carried on playing there too.

The makeshift band was then dismissed and made their way back to E Deck to pick up warm clothes and lifebelts. They reassembled outside on the Boat Deck, near the first-class entrance vestibule. No piano was available here, so they must have been down to a maximum of six players now. These would have been Roger Bricoux and Jack Woodward, cellists, and Fred Clark on bass. Wallace Hartley and Jock Hume played violin while George Krins played viola. Although there is much uncertainty about what they played, that they were playing for quite a while as the ship started to founder is attested to by a number of sources.

With most of the boats gone, those left on the *Titanic* could now only wait for the end, for a watery, bottomless oblivion to overwhelm them. Lightoller was in charge of loading Collapsible D, the only easily accessible collapsible left. Despite the situation, he had the greatest difficulty in finding women. When he asked if there were any around, someone replied: 'There are no women.' The boat, which was the last one to actually be lowered, was almost full. There were lots of Americans nearby, all of whom gave assistance. Some men got in, seeing the space, but then more women appeared so they got out again.

Colonel Gracie had been on the Boat Deck with Lightoller. A frantic search for more women passengers found none. There was now a marked list to port and Gracie feared that the ship was about to capsize. Lightoller, repeating the instructions of Chief Officer Wilde, ordered all onboard to move to starboard to try and even the weight up. (Another witness, Samuel Hemming, also saw Captain Smith telling those left aboard to move to starboard. It is not clear if these are two separate events or the same event confused). Gracie reflected pensively back over his life, feeling that his end was now a certainty.

As they moved to the starboard side a large crowd has assembled by the rails. They included John Thayer and George Widener. Gracie also saw to his horror Mrs Caroline Brown and Miss Edith Evans suddenly appear. Miss Evans told how she had got separated from her friends in the crowd (she now gave Gracie, previous to that night a stranger, her name for the first time). Gracie in the meantime noticed the crew trying to lower a collapsible from the roof of the officers' quarters.

Other passengers prepared themselves for the end. Benjamin Guggenheim, dressed in his best, passed on a message to Steward Johnston: 'Tell my wife if it should happen that my secretary and I go down and you are saved, tell her I played the game out straight and to the end. No woman should be left aboard this ship because Ben Guggenheim was a coward.' He asked Johnson to tell his wife that his last thoughts were of his wife and his daughters, conveniently ignoring the presence of his mistress in a nearby lifeboat.

Perhaps though this was a time to ask for forgiveness, a formal kind of confession now that the end of life was near. One of those aboard the ship as she neared her end was a man called J.H. Rogers, though he was not registered under that name. He was a card sharp but at the end he was helping women into the boats. To one of these he handed a note, saying laconically 'if saved, inform my sister, Mrs F.J. Adams of Findlay Ohio, lost'. His mother broke down when informed of his fate. She had not heard from him for two years, his last known location being London.

As Lightoller was trying to lower Collapsible D, he was 'rushed' by third-class passengers and drew his pistol to make them leave the boats they had entered. There was still some room as a crew member now approached asking Mrs Brown and Miss Evans to enter the boat. Gracie led them back towards the port side. As he did so, a line of crew barred his progress.

As the two ladies approached the boat, Miss Evans insisted that Mrs Brown got in first. However, Miss Evans was then unable to enter the boat. There was a 4-foot-high gunwale to climb and Miss Evans could not do it. It appears that she lost her nerve. She said 'never mind, I will go on a later boat' and then ran away and was not seen again. Lightoller later insisted that when he lowered the last boat, there were no women on deck. Gracie confirmed this saying, 'Neither the second officer not I saw any women on the deck during the interval thereafter of fifteen or twenty minutes before the great ship sank.' But there were 106 women left somewhere who went down with the ship.

Lightoller believed that a couple of 'Chinese' stowed away in the boat; 'foreigners' unscrupulously trying to save their lives being a constant feature of this very Anglo-Saxon drama. By now, he could see water coming up the stairway that led to the Boat Deck. There seemed little more he could now do, having conscientiously if not always efficiently overseen the loading of the boats. Chief Officer Wilde suggested that Lightoller take command of the collapsible when it was lowered. 'Not damn likely' came the reply.

Among those who got off in the boat were Quartermaster Arthur Bright who had been firing the rockets along with Quartermaster Rowe and Fourth Officer Boxhall. Bright had later gone up to the Boat Deck, where the collapsibles were stowed on the deck until they could be put in the davits after the lifeboats had been launched. He had helped launch C on the starboard side and then returned to D on the port side where he was fortunate enough to find a place.

Seaman William Lucas was also in the boat. He could see that there was not long left now. However, he could also spot some way off a faint red light, the sidelight of a distant ship that was obviously now not going to come to help. He could see the hint of a masthead light, perhaps 9 miles away. The water was up to the bridge by the time the boat was launched. John Hardy, a second-class steward, saw that by the time the boat reached the water there was a heavy list to port. He recalled speaking to Murdoch a good half an hour before he left; Murdoch already thought that the ship was a goner back then.

When they left there were no women or children to be seen on the deck. There were not even any male passengers left according to Hardy, which does rather conflict with Gracie's account of many passengers gathered by the rails. It also contradicts Lightoller's recollection that there was a significant crowd on the deck now. He had ordered a cordon to be formed of crew and 'reliable' passengers to stop the boat being rushed.

When Hardy was asked where the missing 1,500 people were by Senator Fletcher at the American Inquiry that later followed, he said: 'They must have been between decks or on the deck below or on the other side of the ship. I cannot conceive where they were.' The boat, including a number of Middle Eastern women, was now lowered about 40 feet into the water.

One passenger, Frederick Hoyt, was picked up from the sea by the collapsible. His wife was already in the same boat. Hoyt had just seen Captain Smith who had suggested that he go down to A Deck to see if there was a boat nearby. Hoyt did as the Captain suggested, saw D about to be lowered and decided to swim out to her. It therefore appears to have been a complete fluke that his wife was onboard.

Hugh Woolner also made his way to a deserted A Deck along with

Mauritz Björnström Steffanson. By now the lights were glowing red. He said: 'This is getting to be rather a tight corner. I do not like being inside these closed windows. Let us go out through the door at the end.' They walked out on deck, and as they did so the water rolled over their feet. They both hopped onto the gunwale, preparing to jump; otherwise they would have been trapped against the ceiling and would have undoubtedly died. The list was quite great by now as there was a 9-foot gap between the ship and the boat.

Collapsible D was just then being lowered. Woolner saw there was a gap in the bows and suggested to Steffanson that they should jump into it. Steffanson jumped in first, somersaulting into the boat. Woolner landed half in the water. Steffanson was standing up and pulled him in. After his rescue, Woolner would proudly tell how he had pulled men, 'foreign' steerage passengers, out of another boat that had previously been lowered. He did not explain what moral difference if any there was between getting into a boat when it was on deck and jumping into one when it was being lowered.

The wireless operators had continued to do everything they could to get help as quickly as possible. When Bride had been running his errands to Captain Smith, he had noticed the lifeboats being loaded. As the ship's situation worsened, the wireless had weakened. Then the Captain had put his head in the cabin to tell them that the engine rooms were starting to fill with water and that it could only be a matter of time before the dynamos no longer worked. Word was passed on to the *Carpathia*.

At one stage a woman had entered the shack and fainted. The wireless operators revived her with a glass of water and sat her in a chair. Her husband then came in and took her away. Bride then went outside where the water was now almost up to the boat deck. Even now, Phillips continued to keep the wireless going. Bride went back to his cabin to get his lifebelt and also extra clothes to keep him warm. He then went back to the operating room and put a lifebelt on Phillips while he continued to work. Phillips asked him to go outside and see if there were any boats left. He himself had been out not long before and came back seeing that things looked 'very queer'. Bride took this to mean that 'the sooner we were out of it, the better'.

Bride did so and saw about twelve men trying to get a collapsible from a position near one of the funnels. It was the last boat left. Bride went to help them and then went back to the wireless cabin to tell Phillips that all the boats were now gone. Then Captain Smith came in for one last time. He told them both, 'Men, you have fully done your duty. You can do no more. Abandon your cabin. Now it's every man for himself. You look out for yourselves. I release you. That's the way of it at this kind of time. Every man for himself.' Only when the water started coming into the wireless shack did Phillips and Bride abandon it. Bride related how, at this last moment, a stoker crept into the cabin and took the lifebelt off Phillip's back. There was a scuffle and the stoker ended it lying on the floor unconscious, or possibly even dead. It has the feel of a story made up for the benefit of a media hungry for sensational tales, with Bride's assertion in the *New York Times* that he hoped the stoker was killed and that he would rather the assailant had walked the plank or stretched a rope with his neck having a particularly grating note to it.

Bride and Phillips made their way out on deck, where the junior operator noted that there were still some passengers without lifejackets on. It was presumably now, or shortly after, that Bride saw Captain Smith for the last time, as he claimed later that he saw the Captain dive off the bridge and into the sea (Lightoller recalled seeing him for the last time, presumably shortly before this, walking across the bridge). The band was still playing, ragtime as Bride remembered it later. Phillips ran towards the stern and that was the last that Bride ever saw of him.

Others had already taken matters into their own hands. Charles Joughin, the baker, could see that there was not going to be enough room for everyone – including him – in the boats and threw about fifty deckchairs over the side, reckoning that they at least would float and give him something to hang onto. He was in the pantry on A Deck, underneath the Boat Deck, taking a drink of water when he heard a crash and the sound of running feet over his head. He made his way out and saw a crush of people moving panic stricken towards the stern as the ship ploughed yet lower into the freezing ocean. He managed to keep himself clear when all of a sudden the ship took a large list to port. Most people were thrown over in a bunch but Joughin managed to keep himself clear.

Sidney Daniels had been helping load the boats pretty much from the start. He had been vaguely aware of the band playing lively tunes in the background. Now all the boats were away save the last collapsible. Someone shouted out for a knife as they tried to cut the ropes which lashed it to the top of the officers' quarters. Daniels took his out of his pocket and passed it up.

Lightoller had climbed back on top of the officers' quarters with a view to cutting down one of the collapsibles from there. There was another seaman, Samuel Hemming, there helping him. Together they cut the ropes holding the boat down and jumped round to the inside, intending to take hold of the gunwales and throw the boat down on the deck. However, the deck was no longer there, as it was rapidly disappearing underwater. There was no chance of lowering the boat now, they just dropped it into the water and hoped that anyone struggling in the water would be able to climb into it.

Steward Edward Brown jumped into the boat and called for the falls to be cut. However, as the water rolled up the deck, he was swept out of the boat and into the water, though he soon bobbed up to the surface because of his lifebelt. He was surrounded by people struggling for their lives whose fight to live was so determined that they tore some of the clothes from him. However, Brown – who could not swim – managed to climb into the collapsible that had by now floated off the ship.

As the end approached, Colonel Gracie was with J.J. Astor, John Thayer Senior, George Widener and 'Clinch' Smith. Once they realized the lifeboats had gone, the situation 'was not a pleasant one'. He recalled the old Trojan hero of school days; *'vox faucibus haesit'* ('his voice stuck in his throat') he reminisced, in a way that spoke eloquently of his classical education. Inwardly, Gracie muttered a valedictory 'goodbye to all at home'. He then learned that there was one collapsible boat left on the roof and decided to try for that.

A crewman asked if anyone had a knife and Gracie handed his over. Some oars were propped up against the officer's quarters so that the collapsible could be lowered down them as if it were a ramp. However, the boat crashed onto the deck, breaking several oars in the process. Then an officer from on top of the quarters asked if there were any seamen left – Gracie believed he was cutting loose the other collapsible boat. Amazingly a couple of the crew were still debating whether or not the ship's watertight compartments would keep her afloat.

Young Jack Thayer was still in the company of Milton Long. They went to the Boat Deck where there was just this one boat left but such a crowd around it that they did not think it was worth the bother of trying to get into it. They then stood by the rail just back from the bridge. There was a big list to port and Thayer feared that the ship might turn turtle at any moment.

As Lightoller moved to the starboard side to see what was happening there, the ship took a sharp plunge forward. Lightoller theorized that probably one of the internal bulkheads had just collapsed and the water was now pouring through the gaping hole that this would have left in the ship's structure. The water submerged the bridge and came rushing up the decks. As it did so, it overwhelmed huddled groups of people.

Sidney Daniels had left them to it and wandered around the deck. He could see that the sea was now almost up to the bridge and it could only be a matter of time before *Titanic* was immersed in a watery grave. 'Time to leave,' he thought. With the water already up to his knees he climbed up onto the deck-rail and launched himself into the sea. He swam out a short distance and came across another man hanging tight to a round lifebuoy. Swimming past this – he thought it was too close to the ship and would be badly affected by the suction when the ship went down – he saw something in the distance. Moving closer to it, he saw that it was an upturned collapsible, Collapsible B.

The wave had swept over Harold Bride too. He was surprised to see that Collapsible B was still on deck. They simply could not launch it. He recalled that 'twelve men were trying to boost it down to the Boat Deck. They were having an awful time. It was the last boat left. I looked at longingly a few minutes; then I gave a hand and over she went.' In fact, as Bride approached to help, there was a sudden wave rising up the deck. It carried the boat off as Bride grabbed hold of an oarlock. It was soon afloat in the sea with Bride firmly attached to it. The trouble was that when it landed in the water, Bride was trapped underneath it. He had to swim out from under her and up to the surface. Here, he would soon find himself surrounded by hundreds of men fighting for their lives.

Seventeen-year-old John Collins, a cook, was on his first voyage and it was turning out to be one he would never forget. He had run across to the port side of the Boat Deck along with a steward, a woman and two children. The woman was in tears. The steward had one of the children in his arms, the mother the other. Collins took the child from the woman and made for one of the boats. Then a message arrived. There was a collapsible being loaded on the starboard side and all women and children were to make for there. Collins was just turning around when the water came coursing on up the deck and washed the child out of his arms. He was then pulled underwater where he remained 'for two or three minutes'.

He came up close to the upturned collapsible. He was only 4–5 feet off and there were people on it already. They did not help him on however; their eyes were fixed on the sight of the ship as its death throes started to convulse her. The bow was underwater and only the stern was now visible. There could only be minutes left before the final denouement.

Gracie saw the wave too. All of a sudden the water swept up the deck and struck the bridge. Thinking that the last collapsible would be overwhelmed by the vast number of people trying to board her, Gracie and his friend 'Clinch' Smith decided to try another escape route. They moved towards the stern and then 'There arose before us from the decks below a mass of humanity several lines deep, covering the Boat Deck, facing us, and completely blocking our passage towards the stern.' The sudden arrival of all these previously unseen people horrified him. Able Seaman Frank Osman believed he saw something similar. He was on one of the later boats to leave (Number 2, lowered about 1.45 a.m.) and could therefore still pick out details on the sinking ship as he was not far off her. He saw that 'the steerage passengers were all down below and after she got a certain distance it seemed to me that all the passengers climbed up her'. He saw 'a big crowd of people' go up to the top deck.

This then was the truth. Hundreds of people had not made it to the Boat Deck, in particular steerage passengers including women. They all moved towards the stern where they found their way blocked by the fence and railing dividing first and second-class. Shocked to the core by the nightmare that was unfolding before him, Gracie saw the water rise further up the decks. It started to roll over him. However, like a surfer he managed to ride the wave and climbed on top of the officers' quarters. Tragically, 'Clinch' Smith disappeared beneath the waters, never to be seen again.

With the end now approaching, some of those left onboard had now decided to gamble all with one last desperate throw of the dice. Jack Thayer stood quietly by the rail, feeling very sorry for himself as well he might. He thought of the pleasures in life he might have enjoyed that he would now be deprived of. He reckoned it was now about 2.15 a.m. and the rate at which the ship was sinking had now noticeably increased. The water was up to the bridge and he reckoned that the bow was now about 60 feet underwater. The crowd surged up the decks towards the stern in an attempt to earn another few minutes of precious life.

The lights now went dull, though they still continued to burn. The roaring of the exhausts stopped, to be replaced by the noise of a mass of terrified humanity believing that the end was nigh. Muffled explosions could be heard inside the ship. All of a sudden, the ship dipped forward. There was a rumbling roar far below, perhaps some of the boilers breaking loose as the *Titanic* was now at an impossible angle. The noise reminded Thayer of standing under a railway bridge when a locomotive passed overhead. Mingled with it were the noises of thousands of pieces of crockery being smashed to bits.

Martha Stephenson saw that the *Titanic* was now well down in the water. There were no lights in her boat (Number 4) and the seaman aboard her did not know how to cast off which alarmed her as she feared they might be pulled down with the *Titanic*. They had been asked to go to a gangway to take people off but it was not open. She was now alarmed as people were throwing things into the water and there was a distinct sound of china crashing. She implored the others to pull away from the ship.

They would later pick up three people from the water. One of them had a flask of brandy in his pocket and was drunk. The brandy was immediately thrown in the water and he was chucked into the bottom of the boat with a blanket over him. The three rescued men told the others how fast the ship was sinking and again Mrs Stephenson implored the others to row out of the danger zone.

Quite what to do now the end was near was an issue that exercised many people in the boats dotted around on the open sea. This was a classic clash between moral values and the instinct to maximize one's own chances of survival. Major Peuchen heard the sounds of a whistle and the boat stopped. Those aboard Boat 6 all felt that they should row back towards the ship to try and pick up survivors. However, Quartermaster Hichens who was in charge would not assent; 'it is our lives now, not theirs'. He had been all for rowing back to the ship when the lifeboat had been first lowered and the passengers had had to remind him that Captain Smith had ordered the boats, when launched, to stay together and row away from the ship. Now he had evidently had a change of heart.

He now ordered the passengers to row as hard as they could so that they would not be sucked under when the *Titanic* sank. In fact, Margaret Brown said that he admonished them all that it was pointless to row away as the suction would be so great when the ship went down; he had apparently lost his nerve. He further told them that the explosion of the boilers would tear the icebergs apart and overwhelm the boat. He reminded them of the *New York* incident when the *Titanic* had left Southampton.

Eva Hart sat in Boat 14, struggling to make sense of what was happening. For a girl of seven, the feeling of terror was overwhelming. There were several moments that would haunt her to her dying day. One of them was the panic from those left onboard after all the boats had gone. Perhaps she could not see what was happening but she could certainly hear it. She felt terrified, not least because her beloved father was somewhere in that mass of humanity.

On the now doomed ship, Thayer and Long were now standing by the starboard rail next to the second funnel. They had decided to jump for it and avoid the struggling scrum of swimmers that would soon be in the water. Now was the time. They shook hands and Thayer took off his coat, thinking it would encumber him when he was in the sea. He sat on the rail and pushed off with both his hands and legs so that he did not hit the side of the ship. It was about 15 feet to the water. As he hit it, a freezing cold got hold of him as if he was in a vice.

Then he was seized by something else, the tremendous suction of the ship as it sank lower. It dragged him down. He managed to hold his breath however and push hard enough to break free of the dying ship's grip. He surfaced about 40 yards away from the ship. He later noticed that his watch had stopped at 2.22 a.m. Sadly, Milton Long – who had jumped just a few seconds later than Thayer – did not make it.

Seaman Samuel Hemming looked over the side with all the boats now gone. He reasoned that he should get off the ship before the panic that would inevitably ensue when the *Titanic* dipped under. Hemming looked over the starboard rail first but could see nothing. However, looking over the port side, he could see a boat not too far off. He climbed down a rope into the water and swam out a distance of about 200 yards to it. This was his lucky night. One of his mates was onboard and held out his hand to help him aboard (this was Boat 4).

Steward Andrew Cunningham had waited until all the boats had gone and then thrown himself into the water. He thought that he was in the sea for half an hour and swam about three quarters of a mile until he was also picked up by Boat 4 which had stayed relatively close at hand (note the difference in perception; Hemming thought that it was 200 yards to Boat 4, Cunningham believed it was three quarters of a mile).

Richard Norris Williams Junior was one of those scrambling to stay alive. He was not helped by a thick and heavy fur coat that threatened to drag him down even though he had a lifebelt on and he threw it off. He also kicked off his shoes and then swam across to Collapsible A some 20 yards away. He climbed aboard, up to his waist he said in water.

All around, the 700-odd souls sitting in the lifeboats looked in disbelief at the sight before them. There, before their eyes, the greatest ship in the world now loomed at a crazy angle. The lights had burned right until these very last moments but they were about to go out for ever.

If for them it was a nightmare, what must it then have been for those still on the terrifyingly slanted decks who waited in terror for the end? The slope of the deck had got increasingly steeper, making it harder for the hundreds still on the ship to stand. Now oblivion beckoned, hidden beneath 2 miles of freezing, black water. Now the terror was about to reach an awful conclusion.

One of the few people to survive from the mass of humanity that now remained on the ship, steerage passenger Carl Jansson, later told how

> we were suddenly plunged into darkness... I could not accustom myself to the change for several minutes. I think I was in a sort of daze and have no clear recollection of what happened afterward or how long a time had elapsed. Suddenly I heard shrieks and cries amidships... People began to run past me toward the stern of the ship, and as I started to run I realised that the boat was beginning to go down very rapidly... Her nose was being buried.

The end of the world was nigh.

8

Descent into Hell

02.18–02.20, 15 April 1912

The awful climactic moment was imminent. Those left aboard the ship prepared themselves for their end. For most, death would come and claim them, embracing them in an icy, suffocating grip. However, there were just a few lucky souls who were about to enjoy a miraculous reprieve but they were in a tiny minority. Beneath the starlit sky, the *Titanic* started to point upwards, a giant finger pointing up to the heavens while her now submerged bows reached down towards the ocean depths far below.

The *Titanic*'s death throes had been long and extended so far. However, most witnesses thought that once the water passed the bridge, everything happened much more quickly. In fact, Joseph Scarrott was more specific. He thought that the decisive moment came when the port light, forward of the bridge, went under and after that the rate at which the ship began to sink accelerated dramatically.

Close to the doomed liner, Jack Thayer had a grandstand view of what was about to happen. Already, the cold was starting to suck the life out of him but he could not take his eyes off the sight of the mighty *Titanic*. She was surrounded by a glare; it almost looked to him as she was on fire. She was continuing to sink lower into the water, which now lapped at the base of the first funnel. Onboard, the mass of those remaining were running back towards the stern which was at an ever-increasing angle.

As the ship sank lower Lightoller dived with it, while Colonel Gracie hung onto to the railings on the officers' quarters roof and was pulled under. 'I was in a whirlpool of water, swirling round and round,' he later recalled. He swam away from the starboard side of the submerged hulk. It was not cold, presumably because the boilers, the fires of which had been extinguished, were still warm.

What happened in the last few moments aboard ship was told graphically by Second Officer Lightoller. Still on top of the officers' quarters, he looked down on the people that still struggled to get away from the deathly grip of the water. As the bow sank down, the stern started to rise up and groups of people started to make their way up the increasingly slanted deck. As he watched, he started to realize with horror the futility of their actions. By becoming part of a crowd they were lessening their chances of survival. Although it was natural to try to hang on to a few seconds of extra life, he reasoned that he needed to stay cool and think calmly if he were to live.

As he rationalized the situation he believed that now was the right time to get off the ship. He dived headlong into the water. As he hit it, it was like being stabbed by a thousand knives. His rationality left him for a second; he saw that the crow's-nest was still above the water and swam for it but quickly realized that this was a foolish thing to do. Instead, he swam to starboard, trying to get away from the ship. He was working hard to make any progress when he felt a heavy weight in his pocket. It was his revolver, now more useless than ever, and he flung it into the water.

Water was now pouring into the stokeholds through a grating. The suction this created threatened to hold Lightoller down. At any moment, he expected the wire cover to break. If this were to happen, he would be sucked down into the innards of the ship and his end would be a foregone conclusion. Just then, a rush of air from inside the ship forced him up, away from the stokeholds. He was briefly pulled under again, but once more broke through, this time for good.

As he reached the surface, Lightoller was aware of many others in the water around him, some swimming, others drowning. He thought it an utter nightmare of both sight and sound. He had come up next to an upturned boat but he made no attempt to get on for the time being and was content merely to hold onto a rope that was dangling over its side. As he watched the black silhouette of the ship rise ever higher he saw more and more people sliding down its steepened decks or plummeting over the side into the water.

Even as he watched, Lightoller saw with horror the forward funnel start to break away from the ship. It had been held by two substantial stays but the immense strain on the *Titanic* now broke the port one loose. The starboard stay lasted for a short time longer but this too then snapped. The effect was to send the funnel crashing over the starboard side of the ship. It fell into the water with immense force, missing Lightoller by inches. Others were far less fortunate and were crushed.

There was however a luckier side-effect for some. The wake created by the funnel falling forced the upturned boat some 50 yards away from the *Titanic*. Lightoller had held onto the rope and now felt it was time to get on top of the collapsible which he duly did. Even at the acute angle she was at, Lightoller noticed that the lights still burned aboard the *Titanic*. At this moment, there was a massive crash, possibly as the boilers left their beds and went crashing down through the doomed ship (though a number of boilers have been found on the wreck still *in situ* in the engine rooms).

A crew member, John Hagan, on the upturned collapsible B along with among others Lightoller, described how the ship starting shaking noticeably when it was part submerged. He looked up and saw the forward funnel falling. It missed him by about a yard. Although the wave pushed them further away from the doomed ship, several of those onboard the boat were washed off as a result. Hagan hung on for grim life but was soaked. Some of the *Titanic*'s decking had broken off and was being used for impromptu oars.

Boat 13 had rowed away from the doomed ship as fast as she could. By about 2.15 a.m. it was clear that the end was near. As Lawrence Beesley watched, the *Titanic* tilted slowly up. She reached a vertical position and stayed motionless. Then the lights went out, flashed back on for a second and then went out for good. There was a loud noise, not an explosion Beesley insisted. It was instead partly a roar, partly a groan, partly a rattle, partly a smash. It went on for some seconds and Beesley assumed it was the engines breaking loose inside the ship now she was at such an unnatural angle.

Slowly but inexorably the bows dug deeper into the water. As they did so, the stern was pulled up, higher and higher, reaching a point until it was almost but not quite vertical. Some of those left on the ship could see that the end was now just moments away and had leapt off into the water rather than risk being pulled under with her. Others, driven by an instinct to hang on to every last breath of existence, clung to the deck rails or had climbed to the stern where they now hung on for grim life.

Lookout George Symons on Boat 1 saw that the stern had lifted out of the water, with the ship's propellers just showing. Nearly all the lights had gone out, and the only one left was a mast light. His boat was now about 200 yards off and rowed further away to escape the expected massive suction.

Elizabeth Shute could see that the mammoth ship was now fast disappearing. Towards the end, only a tiny light was left aboard her, a lantern at the very stern of the ship, the same view that George Symons had. She could not take her eyes off the light, the final indicator that the ship itself had any life left in her. Once it disappeared, then that would mark the end. She watched the black silhouette of the *Titanic* slowly disappear. As it did so, the crewmen onboard Boat 3 urged the rowers to make haste: 'She's gone lads, row like hell or we'll get the devil of a swell.'

To Jack Podesta, the ship had seemed to stay in the same position for a while and he wondered if the watertight compartments might save her after all. All of a sudden, the bow went under and the stern started to rise in the air. Her lights went out and there was a terrible rumbling noise. He hypothesized that it was the boilers falling as well as bulkheads collapsing.

From his grandstand position, Jack Thayer heard the rumble and roar continue to resound around the night sky. Then, as he watched, the *Titanic* split in two. A funnel split off the ship, sending a cloud of sparks into the air. It came crashing down into the water. Jack thought it was bound to hit him but fortunately it missed him by some 30 feet. The suction dragged him down. At the time he must have feared this was the end, but it was not, for as he managed to resurface he came up against an upturned collapsible.

Quartermaster Bright was in Collapsible D. They were about 50 to 100 yards away when the *Titanic* sank. He heard a noise but did not think it was an explosion, more like a clanking of chains. Seaman William Lucas, on the same boat, thought they were 100 to 150 yards away when there was an 'explosion'. Even at this late stage, he saw a faint red light about 9 miles away.

Colonel Gracie was certain that there was no explosion of the boilers. If there was, he is sure that he would have heard it. There was also no wave, which he believes it would have caused. Second Officer Lightoller and Third Officer Pitman also confirmed this belief. Hugh Woolner, another survivor, believed that it was the sound of crockery and loose fittings smashing as the angle of descent became steeper that could be heard. Some of the boilers and engines probably broke away from their fittings too, victims of the irresistible gravitational pull now that the ship was almost vertical.

There is conclusive evidence that the boilers did not explode and it comes from marine archaeology. Dives on the wreck of the ship have identified a number of boilers, all intact and undamaged, some still in position, others scattered loosely across the seabed, confirming that they did not blow up. The noise therefore much more likely came from the sound of collapsing bulkheads and other structural damage.

Lightoller was sure that the ship did not split in two though he confirmed that she did raise herself to the perpendicular. Third Officer Pitman thought she did not break either. Lightoller saw that the after part of the vessel then appeared to level with the water (this does not seem to make sense if she did not split). Then she reached an angle of 60 degrees and the boilers came crashing down. Finally she reached absolute perpendicular and slipped slowly under. There was no explosion whatsoever that he heard but he noticed that the water got markedly warmer.

But Third Officer Pitman heard four 'reports, like a big gun in the distance'. He assumed that this was the sound of the ship's bulkheads going. He believed that he did not hear these sounds until the ship was completely submerged, though this contradicted many other witnesses. Major Peuchen also heard 'explosions' but thought that the ship was still afloat. Fifth Officer Lowe said that he heard four 'explosions' as the ship went down. In contrast, Quartermaster Rowe heard only one sound as the ship sank, which he described as a 'rumbling' rather than an 'explosion'.

It was understandable that, given the awfulness of the situation, people heard and saw different things as the end came. Lightoller's evidence that the boat did not split in two was contradicted by a very detailed description of the end from Seaman Joseph Scarrott, in the same boat as Eva Hart. He described the sight of the last moments as something he would never forget. He had watched as she sank lower in the water with a slight list to starboard. The rate at which she went under seemed to accelerate when the water reached the bridge. When it had reached a point just past the third funnel, there were four explosions which he thought was probably the sound of boilers bursting. The ship was right up on end then.

Then she broke in two between the third and fourth funnels; this was significant as this was close to the position of the aft expansion joint, a point of natural weakness. The expansion joints (there was another further forward) were small gaps, about an inch wide, which extended down just a couple of decks. Their purpose was to allow the ship to flex when the seas were rough.

This was no problem in normal circumstances but the water that had been pouring into the ship at the rate of many tons a minute since she stuck had started to literally pull the ship apart. Again, marine archaeology is a help. The expansion joint has been identified and is now a split several feet wide, evidence of the great tension that was starting to tear the *Titanic* apart.

A piece of the *Titanic*'s steel has also been raised to the surface, and part of it has been subjected to fracture tests. The steel used in the production was according to experts surprisingly strong, almost as good as modern steel would be, and perfectly adequate for the purposes for which the ship was ordinarily intended. However, as the ship started to fill with water she was put in positions she was never designed to be put in. The bow of the wreck shows a number of small, hairline cracks in the superstructure, evidence of the great strains that it was exposed to.

The break-up was a slow, drawn-out process. Modern computer simulation has shown the effect of water flowing into the ship's forward compartments on the structural integrity of the *Titanic*. Incredible stresses were put on the superstructure, especially on the aft expansion joint near the third funnel. The ship would have broken from the upper decks first with the bottom of the ship failing last of all.

The incredible sight that Scarrott had witnessed was a result of the massive stresses she had been under. To make his evidence even more compelling, when the wreck of the *Titanic* was discovered decades later, the ship was found to be lying in two main parts, split at a point between the third and fourth funnels, exactly where he said he saw the split occur.

Others had seen something very similar. Quartermaster Alfred Olliver believed that the *Titanic* broke in half and that the after-part then righted itself for a short time. Frank Osman saw exactly the same thing happening. Olliver heard several little explosions both before she sank and then when she was actually going down. Able Seaman George Moore also thought that the ship broke in half and heard two explosions.

Able Seaman Edward Buley saw the *Titanic* snap in two before she sank; he thought 'the after-part came up and stayed up five minutes

before it went down'. At one stage, he thought that the after part of
the ship settled horizontally and was going to float. Steward George
Crowe was more specific than most. He said, 'Presently she broke
in two, probably two-thirds of the length of the ship ... she broke,
and the after part floated back'. Frederick Scott, a greaser, saw that
the ship 'broke off at the after funnel and when she broke off her
stern end came up in the air and came down on a level keel and
disappeared'.

Frank Evans said that she 'parted between the third and fourth
funnels', leaving approximately 200 feet of *Titanic*'s stern still afloat.
Quartermaster Arthur Bright was categorical in his assessment of
what happened at the end:

> She broke in two. All at once she seemed to go up on end, you know,
> and came down about half way, and then the after part righted itself
> again and the forepart had disappeared. A few seconds later the after
> part did the same thing and went down. I could distinctly see the
> propellers – everything – out of the water.

He did not hear an explosion as she went, more like a rattling chain.

There were then a number of reports, consistent in detail, which
suggested that the ship had broken before sinking. However, despite
the fact that these accounts significantly outnumbered those which
asserted she did not break, the Inquiries that followed decided
that the *Titanic* did not split before she sank. It is noticeable that
most of those who said that she did not break were the *Titanic*'s
surviving officers, perhaps motivated, subconsciously or otherwise,
by a residual pride in their ship. In both cases the Inquiries chose
not to be led by the evidence, perhaps giving excessive weight to the
minority opinion of the officers over other witnesses.

Robert Ballard, who found the wreck in 1985, gave his own
explanation for what had happened, theorizing that 'as the bow sank
and the stern rose ever higher out of the water, the pressure on the
keel became increasingly unbearable until it finally snapped at a
weak point in the structure between the third and fourth funnels in
the area of the reciprocating engine room hatch.' Given the evidence,
nearly 2,000 feet between main portions of wreckage, the absence of
a skid mark between the two pieces and the fact they are facing in
different directions, his view was that the ship almost certainly broke
in two at or near the surface. Probably the Grand Staircase had left

a vast cavernous open space which created a weakness in the ship's structure.

Even more recent investigations have added a twist. These suggest that although the superstructure of the ship did split on the surface, the two pieces remained attached down at the keel. It was only when the ship began her descent to the bottom that the keel section split too. A huge and separate section of the keel has been found on the seabed lending weight to this theory.

All this is of mainly academic interest. Those who were there were not particularly concerned whether she broke in two or not. It was the human drama and its sheer horror that was the greater issue. First-class passenger Philip Mock reckoned that his boat, Number 11, was a mile away when the *Titanic* went down. He last saw her with her stern high in the air. There was a noise and he saw a huge column of black smoke slightly lighter than the sky rising high into the sky and then flattening out at the top like a mushroom. This apocalyptic symbolism, coming from what was a pre-nuclear age, is perhaps one of the most haunting images of the end of the *Titanic*.

Jack Thayer tried to pull himself aboard the nearby collapsible but did not have the strength to lift his legs up. Fortunately, someone else who was already on top of what was effectively a raft rather than a boat pulled him up. The *Titanic* was still afloat, perhaps 60 feet away from him. The forward motion had stopped and it was as if she were pivoting on a point. Slowly but inexorably the stern was rising in the air. The last funnel rested on the surface of the water but Jack did not believe that it broke off.

In horror, Jack realized that he could see hordes of people still struggling towards the stern. They looked to him like a swarm of bees. As he watched, the stern lifted still higher and people began to fall off in ones and twos. She seemed to stay suspended there for minutes and slowly turned as if to hide her end from Jack's disbelieving eyes. As he looked up, he saw that he and the others gathered around the collapsible were beneath the towering propeller. But even as he thought they would come crashing down on top of them, the ship slid gently down towards the waves with virtually no suction.

Margaret Brown was also watching with horrified fascination: 'Suddenly there was a rift in the water, the sea opened up and the surface foamed like giant arms and spread around the ship and the vessel disappeared from sight and not a sound was heard.' According to Charlotte Collyer, the end came with a deafening roar, an explosion. Millions of sparks shot up into the sky. Then there were two duller explosions, as if below the surface, and the ship broke in two before her eyes. The forepart sank beneath the waves and the stern reared up. It stayed in a raised position for many seconds, it seemed like minutes to her. Lookout Archie Jewell also heard several explosions. But Quartermaster Walter Wynne thought that 'she gave a kind of sudden lurch forward. He heard a couple of reports like a volley of musketry; not like an explosion at all'.

Before the lights went out, Charlotte Collyer saw hundreds of people clinging to wreckage or jumping into the water. A terrible sound shot across the waters, a guttural cry of fear and terror at the imminent doom. She tried to turn her face away but an undeniable impulse forced her to look back again. As she did so, the stern of the once great ship slipped quietly beneath the surface of the deep, as easily as if it were a pebble plopping into a pond, taking her husband with her as she went.

Major Peuchen heard 'one, two, three rumbling sounds; then the lights of the ship went out'. She was about to go along with Peuchen's wallet that had been left onboard. It would be picked up from the bottom in 1987 with traveller's cheque, business card and street-car tickets still identifiable.

Now, the huge ship slowly started to rear itself up in its end. Rudder and propellers were lifted out of the water until the ship was nearly vertical. He reckoned she remained there for half a minute. Then she started to slide, slowly at first, then with increasing velocity, until she was at last out of sight, having started her journey to the seabed some 2 miles below. Someone in the boat muttered quietly 'she's gone'.

The end was also described by Mr and Mrs Dickinson Bishop in the *New York Times* of 19 April. They estimated they were a mile away when the deck began to slant slowly up. The lines of light began to point downwards at an increasing rate. Only about every quarter of an hour did they notice the difference. But then the rate increased and 'suddenly the ship seemed to shoot out of the water and stand their perpendicularly. It seemed to us that it stood upright for four full minutes'. Then it began to slide slowly downwards.

As she approached her death throes, the *Titanic* was a beautiful, mesmerizing sight to Harold Bride. Smoke and sparks started to pour out of her funnels. Then she started to turn on her nose. Bride thought she looked like a duck going down for a dive. He still heard the band playing. However, it was not 'Nearer My God to Thee' that he recalled but a tune called 'Autumn'. He was about 150 yards away when the *Titanic* rose up and then finally sank slowly beneath the waves.

Those in the boats could not avert their eyes away from the spectacle, much as they wished to. Mrs Ryerson said that as the bow went down, the lights went out. 'The stern stood up for several minutes black against the stars and then the boat went down'. Someone called out that they should row for their lives or they would all be sucked down. Several of the women, including Mrs Astor and Mrs Thayer, helped with the rowing but there was little suction.

Mrs Thayer, also in Boat 4 which was not far off, saw:

> The after part of the ship then reared in the air, with the stern upwards, until it assumed an almost vertical position. It seemed to remain in this position for many seconds (perhaps twenty) then suddenly dove out of sight. It was 2.20 a.m. when the Titanic disappeared, according to a wrist watch worn by one of the passengers in my boat.

Mrs Stephenson saw the end from the same spot. When the call came that the *Titanic* was going, a cry went up – 'she's broken'. Covering her eyes for a time, she was eventually compelled to look and saw just the stern 'almost perpendicular' in the air so that the outline of the propellers could be seen. She then took her final plunge. Third Officer Pitman took out his watch and noted that it was 2.20 a.m. exactly. As a way of confirming other events, the timing of which may be important, Pitman confirmed that this was based on the same time measurement that had operated on the *Titanic* throughout Sunday, that is it had not been changed at midnight on Sunday as planned. As Pitman pointed out, 'we had something else to think of'.

Steward Henry Etches thought

> She seemed to rise as if she were going to take a final dive but sort of checked as though she had scooped the water up and had levelled herself. She then seemed to settle very, very slowly, until the last when she rose and seemed to stand twenty seconds, stern in that position and then she went down with an awful grating, like a small boat running off a shingly beach.

He detected no suction whatsoever.

An icy breeze blew up, the first noticeable one of the night.

It seemed to herald the last moments of the stricken ship. As Violet Jessop watched from boat 16, *Titanic* gave an alarming lurch forward. One of the funnels went crashing into the sea as if it were a cardboard model, creating a giant roar as it hit the water. The ship then tried to right herself as if she were a wounded animal struggling to get up from a deathblow. Then she went down by the head. The noise was terrific as she rose vertically and then slid beneath the waves.

Of the hundreds left on the ship at the end, the blind terror that they felt as the ship reared up almost vertically was overwhelming. They stared down into a gaping chasm, into the jaws of hell itself, before sliding down into the blackness. Steward Etches said graphically that he 'saw, when the ship rose – her stern rose – a thick mass of people on the after end. I could not discern the faces of course'. Steward Crawford could also see a large number of people gathered at the stern.

Among the few who were there on the ship at this last climactic moment and survived to tell the tale was Olaus Abelseth. He and his two companions, neither of whom could swim, were being forced back towards the stern of the ship. They watched on helplessly as the water crept up the bows of the *Titanic*. Then there was a small explosion, a 'popping and a cracking', after which the ship lurched forward. The deck on which they were standing rose inexorably into the air, becoming so steep that no one could stand. The three of them slid down into the frigid water but managed to hold on to a rope for dear life.

But they all knew that to stay where they were until the ship went under, which could now only be minutes away, would be a death sentence. They wanted to jump but waited until they were just 5 feet above the water. As they hit, they were all pulled under. Olaus had been holding on to his brother-in-law's hand but now involuntarily let go; he thought to himself as he went under 'I am a goner'.

However, his moment had not yet come though unfortunately it had for his companions; he was not after all a 'goner'. He was in the water for fifteen to twenty minutes, though he noticed little suction when the ship went down. He would eventually make his way into the swamped Collapsible A that had been washed off the ship. So too did Rosa Abbott who was thrown in the water from the stern, along with her two sons, Rossmore and Eugene, aged sixteen and fourteen respectively. She reached safety, but they were lost.

Charles Joughin was also on the ship when the end came. When the *Titanic* lurched drunkenly and decisively to port, he knew that she had just moments left. He heard the rending of metal and climbed onto the outside of the poop deck at the rear of the ship and wondered what to do next. Even at this moment when death stared him in the face the mundane intervened as he tightened his belt and moved items around from one of his pockets to another. He looked at his watch; it was a quarter past two.

Then all of a sudden he found himself in the water. He did not jump into it; the *Titanic* simply disappeared beneath his feet. He felt no suction as she went; in fact, he barely got his head wet. He, unlike many others, did not think that the ship had stood up practically perpendicularly before going under but that she had rather 'glided' beneath the waves.

A few others in the 28 degrees Fahrenheit water swam towards Collapsible A. One of the last to reach it was third-class passenger August Wennerstrom and his friend Edvard Lindell. Wennerstrom had noticed Lindell's wife Elin struggling in the water. He grabbed hold of her hand but could not pull her aboard. In the end, he had to let go. He turned to her husband only to see that he too was dead.

Colonel Gracie, pulled underwater when the *Titanic* plummeted into the abyss, thought that his end had come and mentally said goodbye again to his family, praying that they might meet once more in heaven. He said later that, at that very moment back in New York, his wife, unable to sleep, got up and turned to her prayer book. It opened at the page 'For Those at Sea' and she instantly thought that her husband was thinking of her.

He kicked upwards, driven on by a primeval urge to survive. At last, Gracie saw the increase of light at the surface. He tucked a small plank under his arm. On reaching the surface, he found a small crate which he seized; the first piece of the raft he imagined constructing. The *Titanic* had gone but just as he broke the surface he heard a slight 'gulp' as the sea closed over her.

A thin, grey vapour lay over the spot; it 'hung like a pall a few feet above the broad expanse of sea that was covered with a mass of tangled wreckage'. It reminded him of a scene out of Dante. But worse 'there arose to the sky the most horrible sounds ever heard by mortal man'.

He saw several persons clearly drowned close to him. Gracie tried to climb on top of the crate but it toppled over and threw him off.

It was then that he saw one of the collapsibles, upside down, with a dozen men (believed to be all crew) desperately balanced on top of her. Gracie swam over and climbed onboard. No one offered to help him so he grabbed hold of one of the men already on it. Helped up by an unknown hand, he then assumed a reclining position on the boat. This was Collapsible B which would provide a precarious sanctuary for about thirty people in total.

Trimmer Thomas Dillon reckoned that he went down about two fathoms with the ship. He had been on deck surrounded by hundreds of people, most of them steerage. Kicking his way to the surface, he then swam for about twenty minutes. There seemed to be perhaps 1,000 people around him in the water. He saw the ship sink and then the after-part bob up again for a short time. He eventually managed to make it to Boat 4, where he fell unconscious. When he awoke, there were two dead bodies on top of him, one of whom was identified as Able Seaman William Lyons.

Storekeeper Frank Prentice was on the *Titanic* when she sank. He had been one of the many who hardly noticed the bump when the ship struck the berg. He had then stood around, casually smoking cigarettes as the ship's list got progressively worse. Seeing that she was doomed to sink, he had made his way to the stern of the ship along with hundreds of other people left aboard. He noticed the crowd singing hymns as the end approached.

He had hung from the rail, estimating that he was now about 75 feet above the water. Then he let go and fell into the water. It cut him like a knife, the intense cold chilling him to the core. Prentice had helped himself to a bottle of brandy before jumping; when he was dragged out of the water by those aboard Boat 4 the seaman in charge, Quartermaster Perkis, threw it in the water.

Prentice had not had a drop of the brandy and he thought Perkis's actions were reckless. Perkis was worried that some of the people in the boat, already nearly hysterical, would go completely over the top if they got hold of alcohol. However, Prentice later remarked that several people were pulled from the water and died of exposure and he could not help thinking that the brandy might have been the difference between life and death for these poor souls.

There were now hundreds of people in the water, fighting for their lives. The ship had gone and all that was left was the struggle to survive. There were lifebelts for all of those onboard and most people had managed to get one on. However, that was not the problem; the life-sapping cold was the issue. Most people could expect to live only for minutes in these temperatures. Their only hope was that some of the half-empty lifeboats in the vicinity might come to their rescue. For nearly all of them, these hopes were to be cruelly dashed.

9

The Survival Lottery

02.21–04.00, 15 April 1912

Ships were, unseen, on their way to help. To the west, the *Mount Temple* was making her way towards the reported SOS position. By about 3.00 a.m., she had met the ice. Captain Moore had put on extra lookouts, including one in the bow. Not long after reaching the ice, something loomed ahead out of the darkness. Suddenly they saw a schooner coming the other way – from the direction of the now submerged *Titanic* – showing her green light as she passed by. Captain Moore, on the bridge of the *Mount Temple*, could also hear the sound of her foghorn as she moved on by.

It is odd in all the debates about the *Californian* that more has not been made of this schooner. She was according to Moore coming from the direction in which the *Titanic* had recently been. At the time he spotted her, 3.00 a.m., he estimated that she was about 12½–13 miles from the *Titanic*. It is highly likely then that she was much closer, and within sight, when the great ship went down, though Moore thought that she was going at just a couple of knots.

This surely is conclusive proof that there was at least one other vessel in the vicinity of the *Titanic* that night apart from the *Californian* though just how close she actually was must be the subject of conjecture. However, Fourth Officer Boxhall was convinced that he also saw a white light and that he would not expect to see on a sailing ship such as Moore had spotted but only on a steamer.

Moore was now about 14 miles from *Titanic*'s reported position. He could also see a steamer on his port bow, a 'foreign' ship he thought, going ahead of the *Mount Temple*. He thought he could see the same ship when dawn broke. By 3.25 a.m. however, Moore felt that the ice was too thick to push on through and slowed right down. This was a substantial ice-field to his east, which Moore thought was about 6 miles wide and 20 miles long.

It was at about 3.30 a.m. that someone in the *Titanic*'s scattered lifeboats saw yet another light appear upon the far horizon to the south, 'a faint, faraway gleam' as it was described. However, this one got bigger until it was clear that this was a man-made beacon of some description. Then there was a dull, muffled explosion far away. One of the sailors aboard thought it was a cannon but it was not. It was a distant rocket fired from a rescue ship. Soon a single light appeared and then, shortly afterwards, another, lower, just as hoped.

There was now no doubt about it; it was help on its way. The occupants of Boat 13 looked for something to light to attract the attention of the ship. Someone found a letter in their pocket and a match was put to it to create a makeshift torch. It did not last for long before it spluttered out but by its flickering illumination Lawrence Beesley saw something for the first time that night that sent shivers coursing down his spine; tiny lumps of ice in the water, a poignant reminder of why there were sitting in a lifeboat in the North Atlantic at 4.00 a.m. on an April morning.

As the temporary light was extinguished, the rescue ship in the distance also seemed to come to a halt. At 3.16 a.m. *Carpathia* time Rostron had reckoned he had about 12 miles to go to the SOS position. At 3.30 a.m. he had gone half-speed ahead, then slow. At about 4.00 a.m. he stopped.

The *Carpathia* had come up against the ice too and had negotiated her way safely through it. For the commander of the rescue ship was not only a brave man, he was a prudent one too. Somewhere nearby another captain lay beneath the icy water, brave no doubt but certainly not prudent. Just a few miles away too was another sea-captain whose prudence was undoubted but whose judgment, many would suggest, should be under question.

While these extraordinary events were being played out, the pace of life aboard the *Californian* was as sedentary as it had been all night. Between the two of them, Stone and Gibson had watched eight rockets appear beneath the stars. At last, Stone saw the nearby ship disappearing to the south-west of the *Californian*. He had tried repeatedly to make contact with the Morse lamp but had failed utterly. Now thinking that the ship was on its way towards port, he told Gibson to report to Lord what was happening.

It was about 2.00 a.m. *Californian* time when Stone thought he saw the ship disappearing at a rate of knots. He could just see her stern light. The *Californian* had swung around considerably now and was pointing WSW. He told Gibson to tell Lord that the ship had fired eight rockets and was now out of sight. He noted to himself that the rockets seemed to have been moving in the same direction as the ship he had been watching.

As a matter of interest, Second Officer Lightoller, when later asked how many rockets had been fired from his ship that night, said 'about eight'. In the interest of balance, and also to demonstrate how murky many of the details from that night are, Third Officer Pitman recalled seeing a dozen. Boxhall, who was firing them off, recollected that he had sent up between half a dozen and a dozen.

Gibson went to pass the message on to Lord. Shortly afterwards he was back. He said to Stone that he had told Lord that they had tried to contact the other ship repeatedly and had got no answer. Lord had then asked if the signals were all white. At 2.45 a.m. ship's time Gibson then whistled down the speaking tube to confirm that no more lights had been seen and that the steamer was now completely out of sight. He confirmed that the signals were all white and had no colours in them.

These two accounts though are fraught with confusion. Gibson related an account of a conversation that Lord had no later recollection of. Lord later said that he had a vague recall of Gibson opening the chartroom door and then closing it immediately. Lord asked him what he wanted but got no reply and he certainly remembered no discussion. In his affidavit, he did not mention his conversation with Stone at 2.45 a.m. at all.

Lord's inability to remember this 2.45 a.m. conversation was very strange. He was asleep in the chart room but the speaking tube was in his cabin next door. This means that he not only slept through a conversation with Stone but also had to walk from one room to the next while asleep to have a conversation he could not subsequently remember. He then had to walk, still asleep, back to the chart room and lay back down once more.

Then there were the rockets. Several times, it had been mentioned that the rockets were white, as if there was some great significance in this. However, the regulations about distress rockets mentioned nothing about rockets other than there should explode in a star-like display; the colour did not matter. It was a point of some ambiguity; the rules said that the rockets might be any colour – some argued that white was not actually a colour.

However, the star-like appearance of what had been seen intimated a distress signal. There was though something else that did not. Rockets were supposed to make a loud noise when they went off. Neither Stone nor Gibson heard anything on a night that just about every eye-witness said was one of the quietest, calmest imaginable. This was something of a contradiction; they looked like distress rockets but they did not sound like them, having in fact no sound at all. At the very least, it suggested that the rockets must have been some way off.

This though was not the end of the rockets as far as the *Californian* was concerned. At 3.20 a.m. Gibson saw another rocket about two points before the beam to port. He reported these at once to Stone. Three minutes later another one lit up the distant sky and then another. The first was distant, 'two faint lights in the sky' as Stone described it. It was clearly a long way off. None of these later rockets was reported to Captain Lord, though seeing eleven rockets fired off in the night-time can surely not have been an everyday occurrence.

In fact, the time that the *Californian* saw this was about half an hour after the *Carpathia* had fired off its first rocket (assuming the ships' times were closely aligned to each other). At 2.40 a.m. *Carpathia* time Rostron had seen a green flare way ahead of him. It was Boxhall's signalling in the boats that attracted his attention. Rostron knew that green was the White Star Line's night signal. He also knew that he was a good 20 miles off according to the SOS position and the light seemed quite high up. It gave him hopes that the *Titanic* was still afloat. It is noticeable that although Rostron saw this green light, no one on the *Californian* did suggesting again that they must have been some way off.

Rostron had fired off his first rocket in reply to Boxhall's green flare, as a sign that his ship was steaming to the rescue. Just then, he saw the light of a star reflecting off something bright and solid ahead of him – an iceberg. Now he was entering the danger area. From them on he was darting and diving in and out of bergs and small ice. In his own words:

More and more we were all keyed up. Icebergs loomed and fell astern; we never slackened, though sometimes we of course altered course to avoid them. It was an anxious time with the *Titanic's* fateful experience very close in our minds. There were seven hundred souls on the *Carpathia*; these lives as well as the survivors of the Titanic herself depended upon a sudden turn of the wheel.

The rockets were a ray of hope for those in the lifeboats, for they came from their rescuer. Rostron carried on firing them at intervals of a quarter of an hour. As the occupants of Boat 13 peered ahead, the *Carpathia* swung round and showed herself to be a large steamer with all her portholes alight. Beesley saw those lights and, in his own words, realized that they spelt 'deliverance'. Until now, though they thought that rescue was coming, it was believed to be from the *Olympic*. Now, much sooner than expected, they were to be saved from the chill embrace of the early morning breeze and the threat of the ice-strewn ocean. Whispered prayers were uttered and tears freely shed as the wonderful thought of imminent rescue sank home.

The *Carpathia* had covered the 58 miles to the *Titanic's* reported position in three and a half hours, well above her top speed. This in fact gave a clue to the fact that the *Titanic's* reported position was incorrect. A double-watch of crew had been designated to act as look-outs on the *Carpathia*, hoping against hope that they would catch sight of the *Titanic* still afloat. Instead, Captain Rostron had sighted twenty large icebergs, 100 feet or more high. He dodged his ship in and out of them with a great deal of courage, for his ship might easily have slammed into one of the bergs just as the *Titanic* had.

It had not come a moment too soon for those on Collapsible B. Someone there had suggested that they should row for the light of the ship they had seen while the *Titanic* was going down. Then someone else shouted that there was a ship coming up behind them. For some reason, someone checked the numbers aboard; there were thirty people left there. As dawn broke, they saw the *Carpathia* stopped, 4–5 miles away. They also saw four lifeboats, strung together in a line, not far from them, perhaps half a mile.

Jack Thayer had found the water intensely cold. It had washed over the upturned boat constantly. Towards dawn, the wind blew up and it became increasingly difficult to keep the boat stable. Bride continued to keep spirits up with talk of the *Carpathia* coming to the rescue. Between 3.30 a.m. and 4.00 a.m. the lights of the rescue ship were spotted on the horizon (Pitman on Boat 5 saw her lights at around 3.30 a.m.). Thayer was still lying underneath another man, who was crushing his legs.

Fifth Officer Lowe had returned to his small flotilla after his game but disappointing effort to pick up more survivors. As they at last gave up their mercy mission and made their way back towards the other boat, most of them aboard were in tears. But it was now time to think of the living. With the rising of the wind before dawn, Lowe had hoisted a sail. They had been travelling along 'quite nicely' when in the distance Lowe saw the *Carpathia* coming.

Others could see this wonderful sight too. From the start, first-class passenger Mrs Margaretta Spedden in Boat 3 said that the stokers aboard urged that they row away from the ship to avoid the risk of suction. Two oars were lost early on in the haste of departure. Now that the *Carpathia* had appeared on the horizon, someone set some paper alight to act as a beacon for the rescue ship to home in on.

In Collapsible D, Number 14 had come alongside, telling them to stick together. Then ten or a dozen were transferred from Boat 14, which was now very full, to the collapsible and in return one seaman was passed from the collapsible to the lifeboat. Chief Steward Hardy who was on the collapsible had noticed that there were 'Syrians' chatting in the bottom of the boat in 'their strange language'.

Now, as the first rays of dawn signified the start of a day that many thought they would never see, there was no doubt where the focus of everyone's attention lay. Spread out over several miles, the boats inexpertly started to pull as well as they were able for the squat liner in the distance. All looked to the south. Those who had been pulling for that elusive light in the other direction gave up the battle and turned around. Maybe when day broke at last no one bothered to look but, at any event, no one subsequently reported seeing a ship to the north of them. Whatever ship might have been there in the night was now out of sight.